Excellence2FMCG

Manish Sharma

Published by Manish Sharma, 2023.

While every precaution has been taken in the preparation of this book, the publisher assumes no responsibility for errors or omissions, or for damages resulting from the use of the information contained herein.

EXCELLENCE2FMCG

First edition. September 10, 2023.

Written by Manish Sharma.

EXCELLENCE 2

FMCG

STUDENTS & PROFESSIONALS

MANISH SHARMA

Excellence 2 FMCG

A Handy Guide for all FMCG Students and Professionals

Let us come together and begin a journey of FMCG towards global excellence

By Manish Sharma

My Life mantra : Spread the sea of knowledge and raise the bar of wisdom globally.

Copyright:2023 : All rights reserved with Author.

To all professional colleagues to whom I shall always remain grateful for providing useful inputs based on this book is written

ABOUT AUTHOR

An seasoned chemical engineer with MS from BITS Pilani.

A Certified Six sigma Black belt.

CQI & RCA Qualified lead auditor for ISO QMS 9001, 14001, 45001 and FSSC 22000, IMS (Integrated Management System).

Diploma from IIP (Indian Institute of Packaging), Mumbai

A Competent professional with over three decades of industry experience in Flexible packaging, Labeling, Lamination, Chemical Production, Product Development, Project Management, Customer Relationship, Quality Assurance, Technical services.

Skilled in implementation of lean methodologies and 5S technique;

Hold competency in food packaging grade product legal and statutory compliance.

Preface

First edition

Perfection is not attainable, but if we chase perfection, we can catch excellence.

Vince Lombardi

FMCG (Fast Moving Consumer Goods) is a broad category we have chosen; it contains a wide range of products consumed daily by billions worldwide.

Health is one of the top prime priorities for every individual. Everyone wants to keep away from any disease.

We can ensure we have a good awareness of all kinds of products available in the global market.

Why This Book?

The purpose of writing this book is to help FMCG professionals to understand every aspect, whether it is related to understanding the concept of FMCG, FMCG terminologies, food supply chain, food safety challenges, food product market, legal food regulation compliance nationally or internationally, FSMS (Food Safety Management System) certification, food hygiene practices, and many more.

Acknowledgment

Every completed task is the effort of so many peoples. This book is an example of this.

I am thankful to my wife and sons for supporting me throughout writing this book.

I am also grateful to my professional colleagues from whom I got a lot of valuable practical experience incorporated into this book.

Information was collected from many sources such as the Internet, books, and newspapers, attending various training programs, visiting and interacting with customers, participating in the audit process, and addressing multiple technical issues during the three decades.

Since sources for supporting information were not readily available for acknowledgment, I would be grateful to everyone to be part of this journey for their direct or indirect support to make this task possible.

I am also thankful to all for using various illustrations /images to explain multiple concepts better and more clearly and to my friend Dipak Khade for designing a cover page.

If I missed giving credit inadvertently, it will be taken care of in the next version and brought to the author's notice.

CHAPTER 1

What is A FMCG > Basic Understanding

"A brand for a company is like a reputation for a person. You earn reputation by trying to do hard things well."

Jeff Bezos

FMCG(Fast Moving Consumer Goods)

FMCG

Basic Understanding

There should be the query, that when n number of books, articles, and information on FMCG (Fast Moving Consumer Goods) subject round the clock are available over finger touch on the internet in a fraction of a second, then why do these additional sources on the same subject time and again.

Here is a different thought process for writing this book, especially for FMCG manufacturers, retailers, whole-sellers (offline or online), customers, consumers, students, and professionals.

The information available is stored at different locations with different sources, yet there needs to be consolidation.

This initiative will help every one of us to get at a glance all relevant technological, product, and market-related details for our immediate ready reference.

With this, we are now commencing Our journey of FMCG towards global excellence.

Let us come together and join hand in hand in this journey.

This chapter consists of:

> **FMCG Products**
> **Macro Product Categories**
> **Current FMCG Market Trends**
> **Challenges**
> **Technical Dictionary**

FMCG PRODUCTS

Products with a very high consumption rate and non-durable mean having a shallow shelf life. Different product has different shelf life.

The period during which food remains natural by using preservation techniques that inhibit microbiological or biochemical changes, thereby providing a further extension for sales, distribution, and storage, thus allowing time for distribution, sales, and home storage.

By using preservatives, flavors, colors, aromas, and textures, varieties have been added to food products, collectively known as eating or Organoleptic quality.

The aim of doing this is to change the form of food by doing further processing changes to allow further processing (like milling of grain to convert it into flour.

Another aim is to provide desired nutrient quantity and quality in the food for better health (called Nutritional quality).

MACRO PRODUCT CATEGORY

Let us first see what the macro product, especially food products, falls under FMCG, which is primarily classified for our fundamental understanding of all to come at a common platform.

- Snack
- Biscuits
- Bakery products
- Sea-foods
- Dairy products
- Confectionary
- Personal care
- Frozen foods
- Fruit and vegetables
- Beverages
- Alcoholic drinks
- Pet products

Snack Foods

Snack is a part of the food, generally smaller than a regular everyday meal, and it is a light meal or refreshment taken between meals.

There are wide varieties of Snacks consisting of packaged and processed foods. This type of food generally has 300 calories or less per serving, for example, Pretzels, Tortilla chips, Cookies, Cheese, snacks, Crackers, etc.

Snacks

Biscuit Foods

A biscuit is a flour-based baked food product. It is a small baked unleavened cake, typically crisp and flat. It is made up of baking powder, baking soda, or yeast and many other ingredients, for example, Hardtack, Biscotti, Fish and Brewis, Fried, Drop, Dumpling, Soft, Beaten, Scones, Angel, Southern, Herbed, Casserole topper, Cheese & Bacon, etc.

Biscuits

Bakery Products

These products are made from flour produced in a bakery forexample, Bead rolls, Buns, Cakes, Cookies, Crackers, Doughnuts, Pies, Pastries, Pretzels, Bagels, Pizzas, Crumpets, Pandesal, Muffins, Brownies, Croissants, etc.

Bakery

Sea Foods

It is in any form food for humans. It predominantly includes fish, shellfish, and Roe. Seafood is not meat but also not a part of a strict vegetarian diet for example, Fish- Anchovy, Bass, bluefish, carp, catfish, Char, Cod, Flounder, Haddock, Halibut, Herring, Orange roughy, Sardines, Salmon, Trout, tuna, Crustaceans- Crab, Crayfish, Lobster, Prawns, and shrimp, etc.

Sea-foods

Dairy Products

These products are made from milk or directly in the form of milk only. It is received from milk-producing animals such as cows, buffaloes, sheep, camels, etc., for example, Cheese, Butter, buttermilk, Curd, Cream, Milk powder, Casein, Frozen desserts like Ice cream, Ice milk made from dairy products, cultured dairy like sour cream, yogurt, cottage cheese, Custard, etc.

Dairy products

Confectionery Foods

Confectionery is the which is rich in sugar and carbohydrates. Sugar confectionery includes candies (usually called sweets), candied nuts, chocolates, chewing gum, bubble gum, pastillage, and other confectioneries that are made primarily of sugar, for example, Bubble gum, Candy bars, Caramel Carob Chewing gum Chewy lollies.

Chocolate Chocolate bars, LiquoriceLollies Marzipan Medicated, cough lozenges Mints Nougat, Sugar-coated choc bits Sugar-coated nuts, Sweetmeats Toffee Yoghurt compound, Cotton candy/fairy floss Crystallised or glazed fruit and ginger Eucalyptus and honey drops Fondant Fruit balls with added sugar Fruit flakes with added sugar.

Personal Care

With legal definitions, some products commonly called "personal care products" are cosmetics. Cosmetics and personal care products contain a mix of chemicals, for example, Skin moisturizers, Perfumes, Lipsticks, Nail care, Eye and facial makeup preparations, Shampoos, Permanent waves, Hair colors, Toothpaste, Deodorants, Lip balm,

Lotion, Makeup, Hand soap, Facial cleanser, Body wash, Pomade, Hand sanitizer, Mouthwash, Baby products, etc.

Frozen Foods

Food that has been subjected to rapid freezing is kept frozen until used. Food preserved by a freezing process and stored in a freezer before cooking, for example, Peas, Ice-cream, Fish fillets, bread, pizza, sausages, plain chicken, fish fingers, ready meals, breaded, chicken, burgers, ice lollies, Yorkshire puddings, sweet corn, green beans, broccoli, carrots, roast, potatoes, desserts, etc.

Frozen food

Fruits & Vegetables

Botanically, a fruit is a seed-bearing structure that develops from the ovary of a flowering plant, whereas vegetables are another part of the plant, such as roots, leaves, and stems. These are highly perishable with limited shelf life.

Fruits & Vegetable

Beverages Drink

A beverage is any potable liquid drink other than water.

Examples: Tea, Coffee, Beer, Milk, Soft drink, Liquor, Juice, etc.

Alcoholic Drink

An alcoholic beverage: This drink contains ethanol/ ethyl alcohol. Beer, wine, and spirits start with fermentation, the natural result of yeast digestion of the sugars found in ingredients like fruit, cereal grains, or other starches, for example, Beer, Whisky, Rum, Brandy, Vodka, Gin, Tequila, Baijiu, SinganiSoju, Wine, Cider, Korn, Awamori, Cognac, Pisco, Jenever, Mead, etc.

PET Products

Pet foods is a plant or animal product intended to be consumed by pets. It is sold in Pet-shop and supermarkets; It is usually specific to the type of animals, such as Dog and Cat food for example, Crunchy, Soft, Freeze Dries and Jerkey, dental Chews, and Bone like rawhide, Pig ear, human food, Special diet, etc.

Pet products

CURRENT FMCG MARKET SCENARIO

The current global FMCG market is trending towards the following significant factors leading the market.

- Product sustainability
- High health-conscious consumer behavior
- E-purchasing or online purchasing trend
- More income for disposal
- Convenience in the use of products
- High level of consumer product awareness
- The demand for the increasing population
- The high impact of the young generation on the FMCG market
- Increasing consumer convenience to raise attention
- Technological advancement to improve products and services
- Rapid-fire promotion technique and more closeness to the customer

Challenges Ahead

- Throat-cut price competition among big FMCG players.

- Fast-changing consumer taste and rapid ingress of new products, the flood of new products.
- Consumers worldwide have easy access to a wealth of information that provides unprecedented power in their hands, and brands are bound to meet their changing expectations.
- Online shopping by the young generation leads to challenges for retailers.
- Frequent changing consumer loyalty as well as priority.

Technial Dictionary

Here is the description of the term underlined in blue.

✓ Shelf Life: The duration for which any consumable food product remains intact to maintain its desired product characteristics without harming the consumer, here the product is recommended to store in the prescribed storing condition

✓ Organoleptic: These are the different aspects of foods that can be experienced individually by sensory tests via taste, sight, smell, and touch.◈Nutritional quality: It is the value of the product for the consumer's physical health, growth, development, reproduction, and psychological or emotional well-being.

Back to top

CHAPTER 2

FMCG Terminologies > Terms and Definitions

Businesses often forget about the culture, and ultimately, they suffer for it because you can't deliver good service from unhappy employees.

Tony Hsieh, CEO, Zappos

In this chapter, we are discussing the FMCG terminology.

FMCG industries are a sea of millions of products that billions of consumers use daily.

A typical consumer is related only to information displayed about the product and relevant to them.

People working in these industries use a wide range of vocabulary during their interactions, which is challenging to understand.

We have collected all those used terms and definitions and collated them in this chapter for a glance-ready reference to all users.

FMCG : Terms and Definitions

- SKU
- Branding
- Pasteurization and Sterilization
- Primary and secondary packaging
- Contract manufacturing

- Aseptic packaging
- CPG
- RTE
- Bag-in- box
- VFFS and HFFS
- Lap, fin, and hermetic seal
- No look label
- RFID label
- HMA
- Hard & soft goods
- Inert gas flushing
- Stand up and Zipper pouch
- Pillow pouch
- Hot tack
- Impulse sealer
- Laminate

SKU

In this chapter, we are discussing The FMCG terminology.

FMCG industries are a sea of millions of products that billions of consumers use daily.

A typical consumer is related only to information displayed about the product and relevant to them.

People working in these industries use a wide range of vocabulary during their interactions, which is challenging to understand.

We have collected all those used terms and definitions and collated them in this chapter for a glance-ready reference to all users.

Branding

When a product is known by a name given to itself, it is known as branding.

A brand is always a symbol of trust, faith, and loyalty. It has a significant market appeal.

It helps to differentiate a premium product from similar kinds of hundreds of products globally.

Pasteurization, Sterilization, and retort packaging

Pasteurization

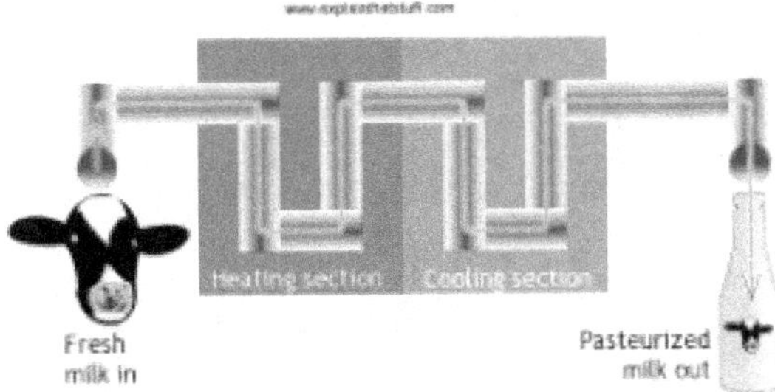

This process is used when food products, primarily liquid ones, are heated to slow down microbial growth.

This process is required for instant heating of the product at a specific temperature for a fixed time, then rapid cooling, and finally sealing.

The taste of the products remains the same.

Sterilization

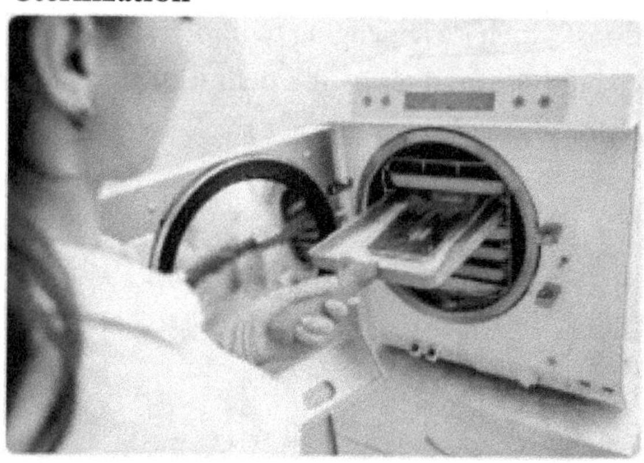

This process eliminates all forms of bacterial growth, e.g., fungi, viruses, spores, and bacteria.

Heat, chemicals, irradiation, and pressure are used for this process.

It is used for all types of solid and liquid food products. It alters the taste of the products.

Retort packaging

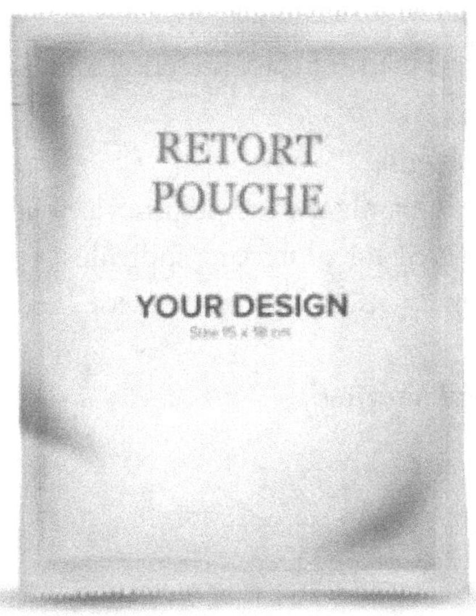

In this process, heat and pressure are used to cook the food in a powerful and sealed package with the convenience of a microwave.

This packaging requires less space for storage and provides better taste in a shorter retort time.

It is less bulky than other traditional packaging.

Primary and secondary packaging

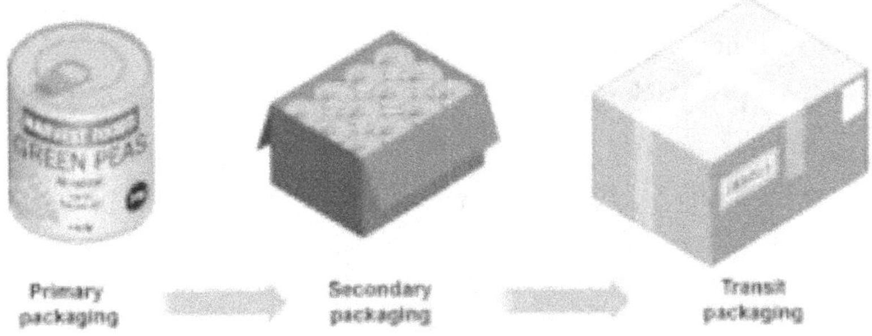

Primary packaging

In this packaging, products are in direct contact with the packaging itself.

This packaging is used for the protection and preservation of the products.

Secondary packaging

This packaging is mainly used for logistics as well as for the display of the brand. It is used for protecting individual units. This type of packaging is generally used in the cosmetic, food, and beverage industry.

Contract manufacturing

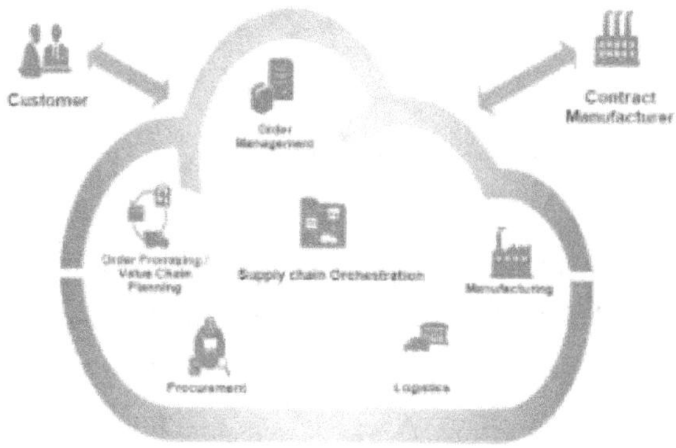

It is an outsourcing process where two manufacturers agree to produce products, components, or parts, which the original manufacturer uses for its following manufacturing process.

Aseptic packaging

In this particular type of packaging, food and other products are separately sterilized, and then products in a sterilized environment are filled into the container.

It is done at very high temperatures, which maintains the freshness of the products and keeps them away from contamination from microorganisms.

CPG

CPG (Consumer packaged Goods) term is used for FMCG also.

It is a low-cost, repeatedly quick-selling product requiring regular replacements, for example, beverages, food, household products, etc.

RTE

Ready-to-eat is a pre-cleaned, pre-cooked, and predominantly packaged product ready for immediate consumption without further preparation and cooking.

Bag-in Box

In this type of packaging, dry and liquid products are packed in flexible packaging and then placed in a cardboard carton.

Products like cereals, crackers, wine, juice, etc., are packed in this type of packaging.

VFFS and HFFS

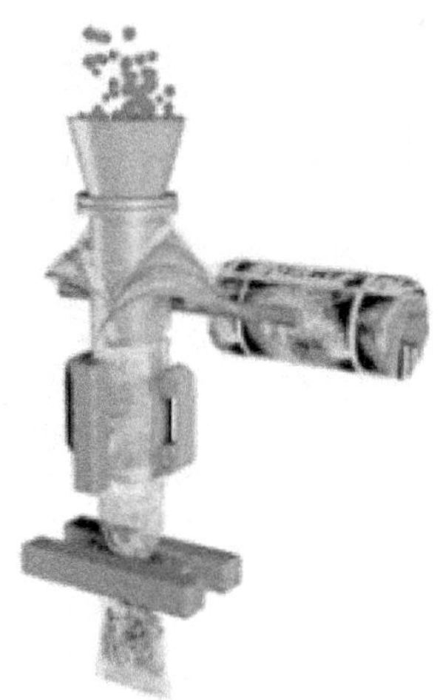

In this type of packaging, there are two types of Horizontal and Vertical form fill seal machines.

VFFS machine is vertical, whereas the HFFS machine is operated horizontally.

VFFS machine requires very little space and is used three, four, and, backside sealing. Mostly machine has a speed of 50 pouches/minute/per lane.

HFFS machine requires space more than VFFS and is used for the zipper, suction nozzle.

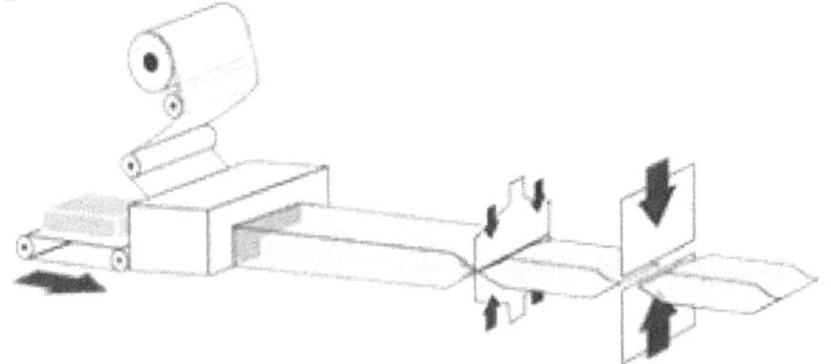

HFFS is more for zipper pouch, suction nozzle, and standup pouch small size pouch. It is a high-speed machine.

Lap, fin, and hermetic seal

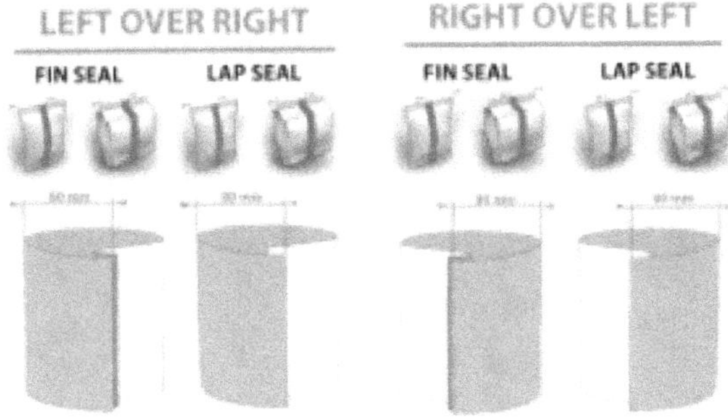

Lap seal

In this type of sealing, two layers of film overlap, or the inside edge of the film is kept over the outside of the film and then sealed together to form the "Lap seal."

Fin seal

In this type of sealing, two layers of film are folded, e.g., inside to inside or outside to outside, and then sealed together to form the "fin seal."

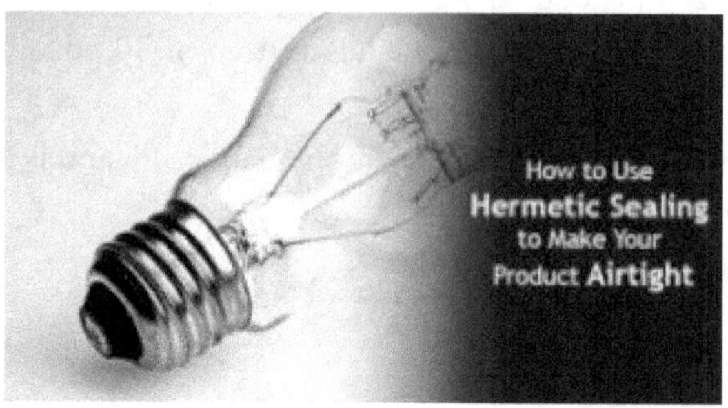

Airtight seal

In this type of sealing, there is complete prevention of ingress of air, oxygen, and any other gases; this helps improve the product's shelf life. It has zero porosity, and the external environment is isolated from the internal environment.

No look label

It is a high-clarity film mainly used in the self-adhesive label application. The label sticks with the container, and it looks like that label printing is done on the container itself.

RFID

It is an advanced technology of bar-coding system known as Radio Frequency Identification. It helps in fast-tracking and retrieval of any item.

It helps store more information and eliminates the onsite reading of the item.

HMA

It is a thermoplastic hot-melt adhesive composed of polymer and resin and is used in wrap-around and self-adhesive label applications.

Hard and soft goods

These products are also known as hard-line and soft-line.

Soft goods include apparel, whereas hard goods comprise a wide range of products, including drink ware, journals, appliances, electronics, furniture, sporting goods, etc.

Inert gas flushing

Various inert gases such as nitrogen, carbon dioxide, helium, or argon are injected into the packaging to eliminate the oxygen from the package.

This inert gas flushing technique is called MAP (Modified Atmosphere Packaging).

This technique is mainly used in coffee, meat, poultry, snack food packaging, etc.

Stand up and Zipper pouch

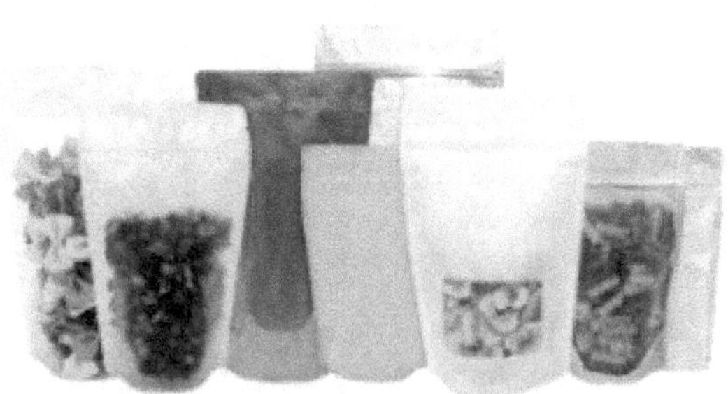

It is a vertical flexible display pouch with a gusseted broad base for self-support.

Zipper pouch

It is a plastic flexible pouch with a molded sealing device with projected ribs inserted for closure. It is a repeated open and closed operation without affecting the quality of the food.

Pillow pouch

It is a flexible pouch in the form of a tube that is sealed from both sides and produced at the VFFS machine, identified by a seal at the top and bottom and a longitudinal seal.

Hot tack

The heat seal strength of the flexible package before the seal is cooled is an essential characteristic of high-speed packaging..

Impulse sealer pouch

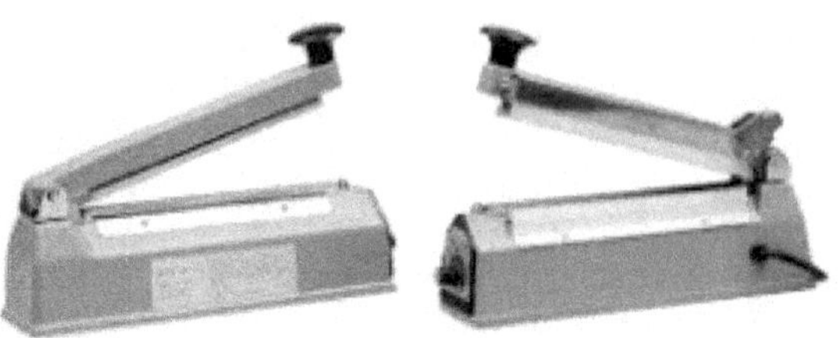

This sealer passes an electrical current through a Ni-chrome wire heating element to seal bags.

It is used in the plastic material for the permanent weld.

Laminate

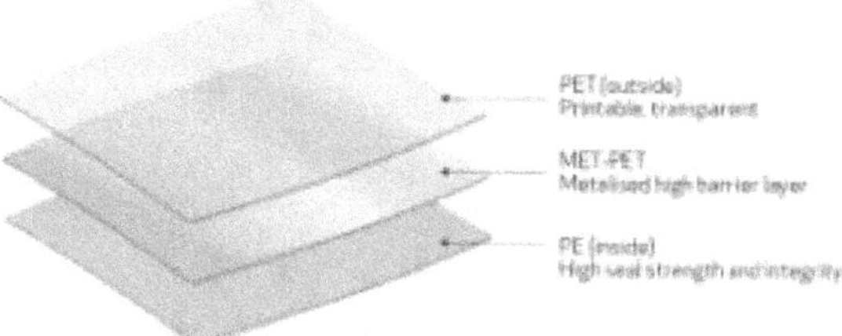

It is a product made by bonding two or more layers of material together to improve the overall characteristics. A combination of laminate is tailor-made specific to product application requirements.

<u>Back to top</u>

CHAPTER 3

Food Supply Chain >From Farm to Dining Table

"We care about every worker in our worldwide supply chain... what we will not do – and never have done – is stand still or turn a blind eye to problems in our supply chain. On this you have my word."

Tim cook

FOOD SUPPLY CHAIN

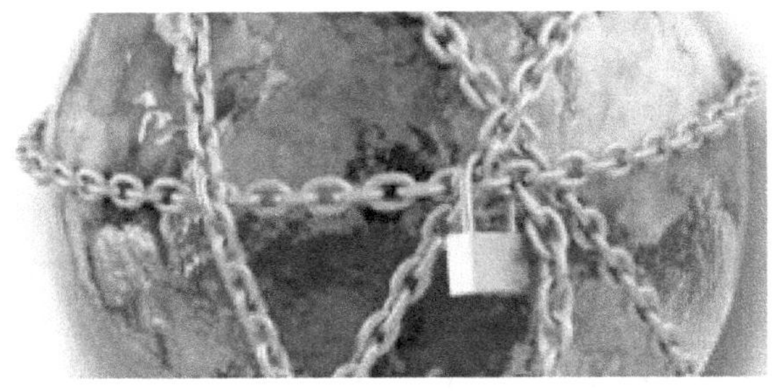

Basic understanding

We know that an extensive range of FMCG products is available through offline retailers, wholesalers, and online shopping.

We do purchase products in the final form or directly ready-to-use for consumption.

We have discussed various macro product categories in our first chapter, FMCG (Moving Consumer Goods)

Before reaching the final hand of the consumer, it passes through the various stages of processes.

Every processing stage adds value to the product stream, from raw material to a refined, high-quality product for final use. With rising consumer product quality consciousness, each value stream becomes more and more quality-demanding to ensure the outcome meets consumer requirements beyond expectation; we may call it delights.

We recommend going through our chapter on Global Good Hygiene Practices before opting for a food selection.

As per Kano's model of satisfaction, every customer delights in due course of time becomes a basic necessity, and this cycle keeps on updating regularly.

In this demanding world, food supply chains continuously evaluate and integrate themselves with changing innovations and technology.

This chapter consists of:

> **Food Supply Chain Concept**
> **Process Stages**
> **Good Hygiene Practices**
> **Food Safety Challenges**
> **Technical Dictionary**

Food Supply Chain Concept

Now let us understand the Food supply chain elaborately :

The concept of "Farm to the dining table" is finding the connectivity of final products throughout the food supply chain and a full-fledged focus on food safety at each processing stage.

Another critical factor that has to be taken into consideration is food preservation as well as safe handling during transportation.

The origins of most of the food products are from agriculture. They are directly produced at a farm or based on farms. Farmers harvest, store, and transport the food to markets or the food processing unit for preservation and transformation into a wide range of food products.

Process Stages

The various process that is part of the food supply chain is as follows:

- Crop, Animal & Fisheries Farming
- Food processing
- Warehousing and cold storage
- Transportation and distribution
- Market and retail center
- Consumer and food services

Crops, Animal & Fishries Farming
Crops farming

It is referred to as an act of producing crops. It cultivates plants for food, animal feed, or other commercial uses.

Broad categories of crops are follows

- Food Crops (Rice, Wheat, Pulses, Maize, etc.)
- Cash Crops (Tobacco, Cotton, Jute, Sugarcane, Oilseeds, etc.)
- Plantation Crops (Tea, Coffee, Rubber & Coconut, etc.)
- Horticulture crops (Fruits and Vegetables)

It can also be referred to as a business enterprise or corporate farming for large-scale production of some of the identified crops for making a good profit.

It also includes:

Radish, Potatoes, Carrot, Pepper, Peas, Strawberries, Spinach, lettuce, salad mix, herbs, Tomatoes, Garlic, Broccoli, Scallions, shallots, onions, Beets, Peppers, Cabbage, kohlrabi, broccoli, cabbage, kale, arugula, swiss chard, cauliflower, cereals (barley, maize, millet, rice, rye, sorghum, and wheat), Tubers (cassava and potatoes),sugar crops (sugar beets and sugar cane), and oil-bearing crops (soybeans, groundnuts or peanuts, rapeseed or canola, sunflower, and oil palm fruit).

Animal farming

It is the other branch of agriculture related to animals that are grown for producing meat, fiber, milk, eggs, or other related products.

It includes daily care, breeding, raising livestock, and aquaculture of fish, mollusks, and crustaceans. Farm Animal has cows, chickens, and other animals raised in an enclosed area.

Farm animals are bred for multiple reasons. We get eggs from chickens and milk from cows, buffalo, and goats. Different breeds of sheep provide us with various kinds of wool fiber, which is finally used for making woolen clothes, from Duck succulent to duck roast.

Fisheries farming

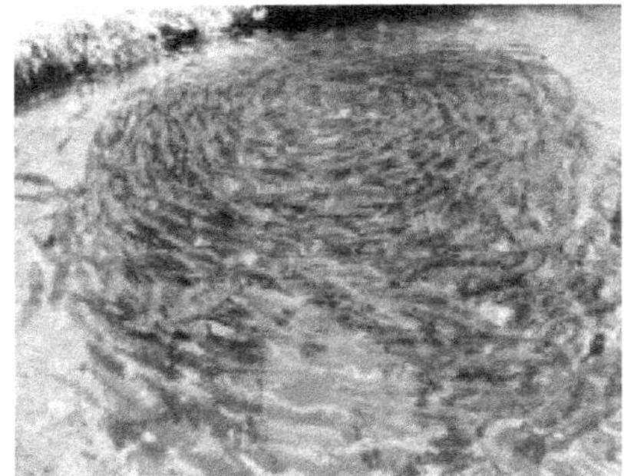

It is a place where breeding of fishing is done to produce on a commercial scale. It involves raising fish in the big jumbo pond called a fish pond; the commercial purpose is only for food, called aquaculture or Aqua-farming.

Marine culture is another way of collecting fish from marine in the open sea.

Food Processing

Food processing

During harvesting and sloughing, most of the foods got contaminated or were likely to get contaminated, which are inedible or have varied physical characteristics.

These require various unit operation processes to ensure uniformity and make food available for next-stage processing.

Unit operations are as follows:

Cleaning

It is wet and dry cleaning; in this operation, contamination (Foreign object) is removed from food and makes food available for the next stage.

Most contamination observed is of the following types:

- Metals: Ferrous and non-ferrous metals.
- Mineral Soil: engine oil, grease, stones.
- Plant Leaves: Weed seeds, pods, and skins.
- Animal: Hair, bone, excrement, blood, insects, larvae, etc.
- Chemicals: Fertilizers, pesticides, herbicides.
- Microbial: Soft rots, fungal growth, yeasts, Colours, flavors, toxins.

Sorting

Sorting is the separation of foods into various categories based on measurable physical characteristics for uniform subsequent processing properties.

The four physical properties are used to sort foods based on size, shape, weight, and color.

Grading

Grading is carried out either by production or QA operators, trained to assess many variables, or the grade of food simultaneously is finalized based on the results of laboratory analysis.

Peeling

Peeling is used in processing many fruits and vegetables to remove unwanted or inedible parts of the product; this helps improve the final product's appearance.

During this process, minimizing costs is one of the top priorities by wasting food as much as possible. The peeled surface should be clean and intact.

There are five primary methods of peeling:

- Flash steam peeling
- Knife peeling
- Abrasion peeling
- Caustic peeling
- Flame peeling

Food processing is the transformation of agricultural, animal or other products into edible food.

Primary food processing is very important to make most of the foods eatable.

Second food processing converts ingredient into useful edible foods.

Tertiary food processing food categories are having high nutrition product having high sugar and salt content with least fiber content.

Primary processing

Primary food processing turns agricultural products, such as raw rice or livestock, into some could be eaten. This type of product category has been produced for thousands of years by drying, threshing.

Winnowing

And it was grinding grain and slaughtering animals for meat.

Along with this, there is deboning and slicing meat, freezing and smoking fish and meat, and extraction and filtration of oil and preservation.

Various technologies are being used for food preservation, such as irradiation, homogenizing, and pasteurization.

To control food safety hazards due to contamination during primary processing, various process controls are in place through the Contamination GMP (Goods Manufacturing Practices), HACCP (Hazard Analysis Critical Control Point), or Process FMEA (Failure Mode Effect Analysis) tool we will learn in later in other chapters of the book.

Secondary Processing

Secondary food processing is the regular process of making food from ingredients that are ready to use, like Bread and sausages, Fermenting fish, making wine or beer, and grinding meat.

Tertiary Processing

Tertiary food processing is the commercial production of processed food ready to eat or heat and serve food.

Warehousing & Cold Storage

Perishable food products include fruits, vegetables, fresh meat, and freshly cooked food stored for later use. It is usually stored in a refrigerator.

Why do we need storage?

Storage is a critical function that involves holding and preserving foods from production until it is taken out for consumption.

The storage of foods, from the time of production to the time of consumption, ensures consistent availability of foods in the market.

Storage ensures that the quality of perishable and semi-perishable products is sustainable from any deterioration that directly leads to food safety hazards.

Some products only have seasonal demand, so storage becomes a basic necessity. It helps balance demand and supply and consistency in product pricing.

Storage is one source of employment.

Methods of storing

- **Refrigeration**

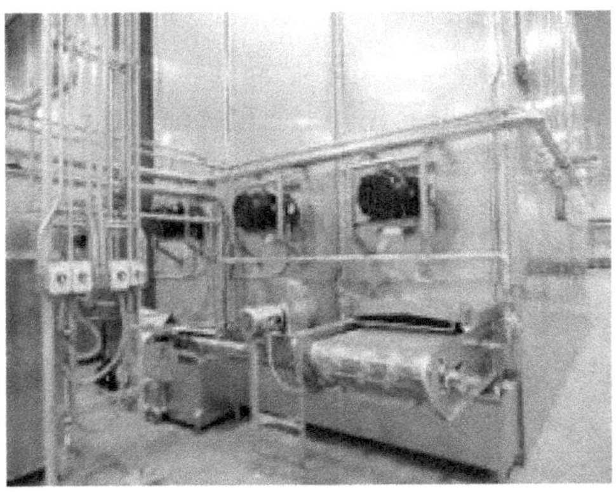

Refrigeration can substantially reduce the rate of food deterioration. Due to low temperatures, the growth of microorganisms and the rate of change in food is drastically reduced.

These are two of the main fundamental reasons for food spoilage.

- **Cold Storage**

Cold storage is essential for preserving perishable commodities like milk, meat, eggs, vegetables, fruits, etc. This cold storage gives perishable food items an extended shelf life by preventing them from rotting due to high humidity, high temperature, and microorganisms.

This results in a substantial reduction in losses due to spoilage.

- **Warehouse**

Public sector agencies are involved in building large-scale storage and warehousing capacities for storing food grains and other items.

Benefits of Warehouses:

It is a scientific storage of products from weather, rodents, insects, and pests. They help in arresting quality and quantity losses.

It helps meet the financial needs of people who store the product by providing value for the goods stored.

It helps regulate the balance of demand and supply of goods in the markets.

It also helps in offering market intelligence for developing marketing strategies.

Transport & Distribution

Distribution

Advantages of implementing ERP system

Advantages of implementing ERP system

It helps meet all food safety regulation compliance at each stage of transportation & distribution; having the highest technologically advanced communication system is mandatory.

Still, there is an old way of communication about specification and time discipline using physical documents and traditional phone calling, which proves ineffective and prone to errors.

Due to these challenges, distributors now look for a whole error-proof system in Japanese TQM terminology called Poka-yoke.

ERP (enterprise resource planning) is a direct solution provider for most requirements. It is a centralized system that all interested parties can access and streamline their quality control processes.

The shipping conditions (e.g., packaging, temperature, and vehicle readiness) required by the customer or according to the food category can be done at a single location.

It helps generate tests, checks results, and records of loading and unloading processes digitally or through other mobile apps.

It has made supply chain manager life easy and helps in easy and efficient accessibility as well as ensuring legal compliance.

ERP system helps improve the overall effectiveness of good & timely delivered quality products at the customer's doorstep.

Timing is a critical, crucial factor in the cold chain. Strict packaging, labeling, and transportation guidelines helped prevent widespread food-borne illness.

Overripe or damaged product is highly susceptible to decay or infection. Fruits like bananas, avocados, etc., are repining naturally after harvest.

Producers and distributors utilize this natural requirement by harvesting these items before they ripen and transporting them to finish ripening during transit.

For these fruit items, adequate transportation and climate control measures like refrigeration and ethylene controls help to reduce the risk of over-ripeness or spoilage in transit.

Market & Retail Center

Market & retail

The retail industry faces tough competition due to the entry of additional players at a regular pace due to exponential growth in this organized market with less penetration.

There is one more reason for low entry and exit barriers, making this market very attractive for new players to enter this niche with a high level of investment.

Now, every player in the market is available with a wide range of similar products, making the market cost-competitive; this is shifting in paradigm from product to cost differentiation.

The player is working round the clock for cost reduction and enhancing logistical competency to get long-run competitive benefits, creating a tough fight for other players in the value chain.

Vendors are prominent in numbers with their self-distribution system, indirectly serving the retailers.

Retailers are also working for self-pickup from suppliers for better pricing. It helped minimize intermediaries, turning into cost reduction and enhancing profits.

The major problem is manual labor dependence work for packing and parceling, increase in SKUs (Keeping Units), brand & high inventory level.

The retail supply chain is highly complex due to the wide range of SKUs, multiple storages and sales locations, and fluctuating and unpredictable markets; this is highly dominating in the FMCG supply chain, especially in the food chain.

Consumer & Food Services

The retail food industry / Supermarket / traditional Grocery stores sell food for either first preparation and then consumption or for direct final consumption (Ready to eat) at home or away from home.

External Hotels, Restaurants, cafeterias, and fast food centers, e.g., McDonald's, Pizza huts, and food courts, are common food business centers that do final preparation and sell the food ready for consumption.

These food sectors are regulated by the state's food safety law.

Any restaurant, tea or coffee shop, cafeteria, grill, sandwich shop, bar, catering kitchen, bakery, grocery store, meat market, food processing plant, or other places where food or drink is prepared for sale or service to the public in the premises is considered as a food establishment.

The bakery produces bread or bread products, cakes, cookies, crackers, doughnuts, and many other products.

Movable food unit, which is run on the vehicle.

A retail food store is where food is offered to the consumer for it is consumed outside the premises.

Consumer education is an essential part of any food chain. Labeling on any product provides the consumer with detailed and accurate information about the product.

The distinction between nutrition, food safety, and promotion is difficult. Mandatory/required information on the label is nutritional information; it encourages the consumer to use the product for their convenience. Both of these objectives need to emphasize food safety.

Today's food service professionals face ever-increasing consumer demands to provide fresh, quality, nutritious food as fast and efficiently as possible at the lowest price, as explained earlier about customer delights.

Continual innovation in food services is the proven key to success.

With the increase in population, there is a steep rise in urbanization and westernization in food taste and content in rising consumers; this is primarily happening in emerging economic countries.

There is a significant increase in food service outlets due to rising spending capacity.

There is a rising demand for food professionals due to their research and innovative ideas in providing fit-for-purpose ingredients in the food they are offering.

Technical Dictionary

Here is the description of the term underlined in blue.

Livestock

All the live animals that grow to produce food products are called livestock. For example, Buffalo, Goat, Chicken, etc.

Aquaculture

It is the growing of water animals such as fish or plants in the water.

Marine Culture

It is the cultivation of marine species organisms for food and other products in the open sea or places where seawater is filled up.

Threshing

In this process, grain is removed from the chaff by mechanical beating.

Winnowing

It is removing the trash from the grain by passing air through it. Grain is dropped from a height, and the air is blown through the grain and taken away from the chaff.

Food Irradiation

It is the application of ionizing radiation to food. This technology improves food safety and shelf life by reducing or eliminating microorganisms and insects.

Homogenizing

It is to treat milk so that the cream is mixed into other parts of the liquid.

Food Fraud

As per FSSC, Food Fraud is A collective term encompassing the deliberate substitution, addition, tampering, or misrepresentation of food, food ingredients or food packaging, labeling, product information, or false or misleading statements made about a product for economic gain that could impact consumer health

Food Defense

As per FSSC, Food defense is the process of ensuring the security of food and drink from all forms of intentional malicious attack, including ideologically motivated attacks leading to contamination or unsafe products.

Poka-yoke

It is a way of fool-proofing the system to arrest any failure due to manual invention.

Pasteurization

It is the partial sterilization of foods at a temperature that destroys harmful microorganisms without significant changes in the chemistry of the food.

Sterilization

Any process that eliminates, removes, kills, or deactivates all life forms (referring to microorganisms such as fungi, bacteria, viruses, spores, unicellular eukaryotic organisms such as Plasmodium).

<u>Back to top</u>

CHAPTER 4

FMCG Industry Challenges > Challenges for Business Sustainability

Every turn has had its challenges, late nights and pressures, but with each comes opportunity. The opportunity to do better, be better or fail forward.[1]

Inoba Siwundla, brand manager at Burger King South Africa

FMCG Industry Challenges

Nowadays, FMCG industries are running on a tightrope for sustainability. Enterprises are trying to remain sustainable by implementing various operational excellence tools and techniques.

There are many challenges that these industries are currently facing.

All these challenges are compiled and discussed in length in this chapter.

Various challenges are as follows.

FMCG Industry: Major Challenges

- Lack of data analytics

---

1. https://www.bizcommunity.com/Article/196/809/190267.html

- Continual introduction of innovative product in the market
- Increasing concentration of supply chain
- Global competitive market
- Fluctuating operational efficiency
- Lack of marketing intelligence
- The ineffective supply chain system
- Inconsistency in product quality
- Organizational model
- Inefficient management of price and promotion.
- Lack of compliances with international regulations
- Delivering personalized promotions.

Lack of data analytics

Every organization has abundant availability of business data. BI (Business Intelligent tools).

FMCG industries depend on data analytics or BI (Business intelligence) tools; this helps provide insight and decision-making, but it may not give 360 views of the whole business process.

Data needs to be collected and analyzed with different tools and techniques to provide crystal pictures of the business and identify the exact root cause to help make correct business decisions.

Continual introduction of innovative products in the market

The innovation rate could be better currently. Despite all kinds of difficulties, innovation is the predominant strategy of any business.

The sustenance of any industry depends on how fast they introduce new products in the market, keeping time to market as low as possible to remain competitive.

Increasing concentration of supply chain

Concentration in the food supply chain is on a growing trend.

Most of the commodity FMCG products are now controlled by major players with a significant pie of their share in the global market.

To lower manufacturing costs, there is a

Probability of compromising with environmental precautions in disposing of waste material produced or looking towards employing cheaper labor.

Global competitive market

Global FMCG is becoming increasingly competitive due to the pressure of sustaining product quality and keeping costs under control. It resulted in cut-throat competition among big FMCG players.

Now, there is a need for the business to look into the implementation of operational excellence immediately to remain competitive on a long perspective.

Fluctuating operational efficiency

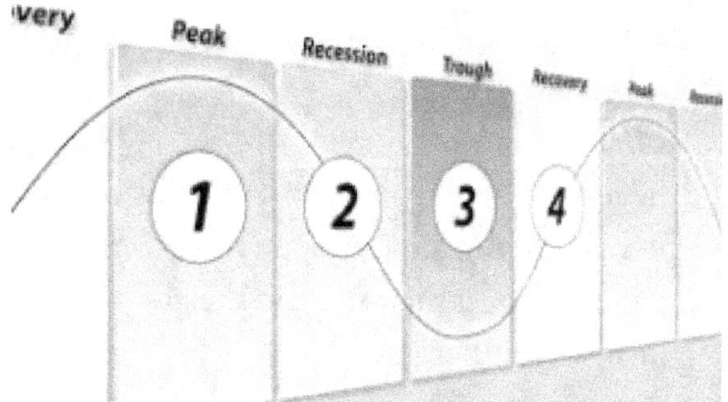

Every FMCG organization has a significant internal challenge to uncover its operational inefficiency and find a way to improve and optimize it.

If it can be done right now, it would positively impact overall profitability and remain noncompetitive.

Operational excellence implementation is the only key to success in enhancing operational efficiency.

Lack of marketing intelligence

The goals of marketing will always remain unchanged. It is essential to understand the customers and their requirements and connect with them.

Every marketing person has to make their customer aware of their brand and know how to connect them with all possible channels.

The diverse, broad, and hard-to-predict influencing factors in sales and marketing make the FMCG business very tough; even after running the proper sales promotion, choosing the best campaign, and creating a cost-effective supply chain, the overall success depends on how accurate and fast the decision has been taken.

The ineffective supply chain system

High WIP (work-in-progress), finished product inventory, and poor warehouse management. Currently, the FMCG sector works with multiple layers of warehouses and retailers between them and the end consumers.

FMCG companies need to connect with the consumer with a well-designed supply chain. Still, it incurs high packaging and transportation costs, forcing them to identify innovative ways for well-balanced logistics costs and better market penetration.

Retailers are now becoming power centers, extracting higher margins from FMCG companies.

FMCG companies need to use modern techniques and drastically improve their supply chain performance to compete globally.

Inconsistency in product quality

Product quality and consistency at the international level play a vital role in sustaining the global market. It is especially critical for a big FMCG brand.

One small silly mistake could spoil the whole brand image internationally, and its global financial impact could be imagined.

Organizational model

There is another challenge in developing an organizational model; everyone has to get accustomed to the multinational work environment.

The organization chart distinguishes actual business from future business; it includes the younger employees who better understand the consumer and excel in the organization in all areas.

Inefficient management of price and promotion

The business needs to get stunning market growth by aligning and optimizing the pricing and promotions.

The organization has to play a strategic role in the market to get the best EBITA result.

Compliances with international regulations

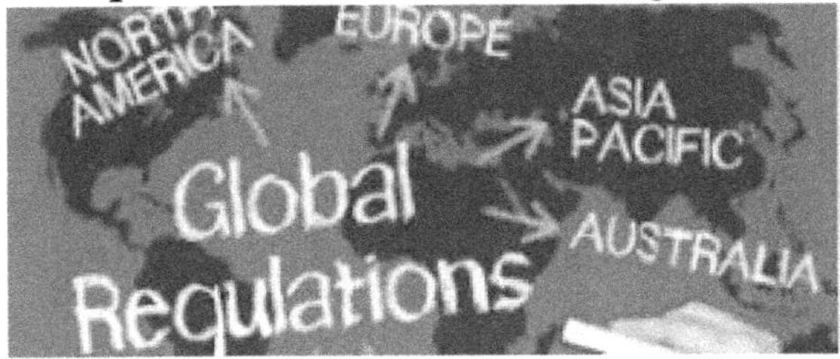

Nowadays, the consumer is becoming more health-conscious, strongly supported by compliance with international and local state regulations.

These regulations are more stringently being followed in the FMCG industry due to the interaction of their food products directly with consumers.

Every FMCG industry must get its products to comply with all the national & international standards.

Delivering personalized promotions

As discussed earlier, retailers are now becoming power centers in the FMCG markets, and whatever discounts they are extracting from the FMCG industry, they are offered as a personalized promotional discount to their consumers.

There is a need of the hour for the FMCG industry to look towards more automation of their process to reach operational excellence.

<u>Back to top</u>

CHAPTER 5

Food Safety Challenges >Basic Concept of Food Safety

Let your food be your medicine, and your medicine be your food.
Hippocrates[1]

Food Safety Challenges

Basic Understanding

Nowadays, it is a growing trend of food outings or less preparation of food at home due to other superseding priorities and commitment, which restrict individuals with no option other than looking for ready availability of ready-to-eat food products within a shorter time and doorstep delivery, for example, Zomato, Swiggy, Pizza hut, Domino, and many more around the world.

It has added a lot of food safety challenges due to the uncontrolled source of incoming raw materials and their quality.

Food Safety Concept

Now let us understand Food safety challenges more elaborately:

---

1.   https://www.azquotes.com/author/22138-Hippocrates

Food Safety is generally referred to the proper handling, preparing, and storage of food in the best possible way to minimize the probability of individuals falling sick from food-borne diseases.

Food safety is now a concern for everyone globally, covering a wide variety in many different sections of everyone's life.

Predominantly, it aims to prevent food from getting contaminated and cause food-related issues, such as food poisoning.

Different methods and techniques achieve it. For example, properly cleaning, sanitizing all contact surfaces, processing equipment, and other pots.

Implementing best hygiene practices, effective pest control systems, and a safe work environment are the key to success in food safety.

Major Challenges

> Change in lifestyle
> Evolving biological risks
> Challenges associated with processed and pre-packaged food
> Inadequate literacy level about nutrition & food safety
> Excess consumption of nutrients or other food ingredients
> Increased consumer dependency on digital services or dietary choices
> Food-fraud
> Food-defense
> Bioterrorism
> Imported food products.
> Climatic change.
> Increasing the concentration of the supply chain
> Food allergen

Let's discuss and understand each global challenge.

Change in lifestyle

In the present world, we spend much more of our days feasting out at cafés than we did previously. In the old generation, eating out would probably be an uncommon treat; put something aside for exceptional events.

Nowadays, numerous families are eating out on a weekly or some time before that. Furthermore, you'll probably accumulate more calories when you eat out than at home.

This expanding pattern of eating out is growing; people are becoming more overweight and inviting health-related issues.

Evolving biological risks

Out of four significant hazards, e.g., Physical, chemical, biological, and allergen, biological is one of the major concerns as it can not be detected directly by the naked eye.

We can classify biological hazards by the contamination of microorganisms in food items.

It is present in the air, food, water, animals, and the human body; these harmful microorganisms create food-borne diseases.

There are various types of biological hazards found in multiple products

Salmonella: Meat, Poultry, juice, fruit, eggs, unpasteurized milk, cheese, fruits, vegetables, nuts, and spices.

E.coli: Uncooked fruits, vegetables, meat, unpasteurized milk, cheese, etc.

Norovirus: RTE (Ready to eat) foods, shellfish, etc.

Listeria: Hot dogs, Ready-to-eat deli meats and hot dogs, unpasteurized milk or juice, unboiled milk.

Campylobacter: Raw and undercooked poultry, unpasteurized milk, contaminated water.

Challenges associated with processed and pre-packaged food

Buying processed foods leads to individuals eating more than the suggested measures of sugar, salt, and fat as they may need to learn what amount is in the food they are purchasing and eating.

These foods can likewise be higher in calories because of the high measures of included sugar or fat, high in sugar content.

- The product packaging is designed for excess consumption.

- Artificial ingredients are added to the product to enhance shelf life and taste.

- People are becoming habitual with junk food.

- The product generally contains high carbohydrates.

- The product has low nutrient content.

- The product has low fiber content.

- It is easy to digest.

- It contains high transfats

If these are in products, it leads to increased obesity and illness.

Inadequate literacy level about nutrition & food safety

It is one of the significant challenges globally to have a low literacy level on nutrition and food safety.

There is a proper need for communication about health communications and health literacy, affecting consumer knowledge and behavior regarding food safety, nutrition, and other health matters.

Food literacy in other broader contexts is food well-being; it provides physical but also emotional and psychological nourishment.

Knowledge about food safety requirements will improve the quality of consumption choices.

There are three basic requirements, i.e., Conceptual knowledge, Individual level literacy, and motivation for active participation.

Excess consumption of nutrients or other food ingredients

some ingredients are extra in many foods, including breakfast cereals and beverages. Due to that, we take more than prescribed; the excess is only sometimes ok as one side is more expensive, and there is every chance of side effects.

Excess of Vitamin A causes liver damage, bone weakening, headache, etc.

Excess Omega-3 fatty acids intake creates blood thinning problems.

An excess amount of cinnamon contains coumarin, which may be harmful if taken in excess.

Nutmeg provides flavor to meals, but when used in excess may cause poisoning.

The active ingredient in regular coffee is caffeine, but an intake above 400 to 600 mg may cause overwhelm the nervous system, causing insomnia, nervousness, and irritability.

Brazil nuts contain selenium, but excess intake could be toxic.

So it is necessary to take nutrients and other food ingredients as prescribed only to avoid any side effects which might turn into a severe health concern.

Food fraud

Food fraud is the demonstration of deliberately adjusting, distorting, mislabeling, substituting, or altering any food item anytime along with the farming to the dining table.

Misrepresentation can happen in the raw material or call it ingredients, in fixing, in the final food product, or the food packaging.

Deliberate substitution, weakening or expansion to a raw material or food item, or distortion of the material for monetary profit (by expanding its evident worth or lessening its expense of generation) or to make hurt others (by noxious tainting) is 'Food fraud.'

Food fraud is the trickiness of buyers through the deliberate deformation of food.

- By substituting one item for another.

- Utilizing unapproved upgrades or added substances

- Distorting something (e.g., nation of source)

- Misbranding or forging

Food defense

It is the procedure adopted to prevent any malicious interference of foreign objects in raw material or final product that harms health.

It protects food products from intended contamination by physical, biological, chemical, or any radiological introduction to cause harm.

Food defense is the better word is intentional contamination by any company or competitor employee for damaging the company's brand image, causing large-scale product recall and financial trouble, but no intention to create mass-scale public illness.

People of this kind are aware of product manufacturing procedures and know the CCP (Critical Control Points); failure to comply leads to a mess.

Bio-terrorism

It is the intentional contamination of harmful bio-organism in food products to affect humans or some other living body at a large scale, termed bioterrorism.

The intentional release of viruses, bacteria, or other germs in food products leads to sick or killing people, livestock, or crops.

It would not be wise to share any such type of detail. Imported food products.

Importers must ensure that foreign suppliers who manufacture the food products comply with all food safety-related legal requirements for exporter and importer nations.

The following are essential requirements for importing food products to ensure good quality.

- License/Registration required for import of food.
- Shelf Life of Imported Food
- Packaging and Labeling of Imported Food
- Food Sampling and Analysis, no objection Certificate/ Non-conformance Certificate

Climatic change

Climate change is impacting food safety resulting in malnutrition. Safe and utterly nutritious food is vital in addressing this issue.

Another impact of climate change on the availability of secure food is being discussed on the global platform and is an area of interest for research.

Microorganisms like bacteria and viruses can survive at higher temperatures and humidity levels and grow exponentially.

Many food-borne pathogens like Salmonella grow very fast in such favorable climatic conditions.

There is an emergence of new biological hazards due to frequent changes in crop technology to improve productivity.

Pathogen is becoming more and more antibiotic-resistant due to the use of medicine for farm animals.

Nowadays, the use of various range of chemicals in crop manufacturing processes creates a wide range of food safety issues due to the presence of toxins.

If we see at ocean aquaculture, there is a significant risk of a high concentration of bio-toxin in fish. After consumption, it would finally impact the health of the human being.

Increase in concentration of the food supply chain.

The concentration of the food supply chain is on a growing trend. Major players are controlling most of the commodity FMCG products with a significant pie of their share in the global market.

For example, three to four players control around 40 % coffee market. In contrast, a similar no. of companies, in comparison to millions of producers and consumers on either side of the chain, controlled 70 to 80 % of tea globally; the same applies to food and beverage, confectionery, etc.

There is also the domination of food retailing by Supermall like Walmart, Metro, and many more.

Food safety and traceability requirement has shifted control production operation to the extensive farming house.

For lowering manufacturing costs, there is a probability of compromising with environmental precautions in disposing of waste material produced or looking towards employing cheaper labor.

It creates a lot of risk and uncertainty that producers could act to downgrade product quality or decrease research and innovation exercises due to a lack of funds.

Legal bodies globally have taken several initiatives to address this excessive buying power for the benefit of farmers /producers.

Food allergens

Allergens are mostly proteins base substances that naturally occur in foods, and their derivatives may cause grave concern to the immune response system.

When our immune system attacks protein, it is termed a food allergy. Our method produces a protein called IgE antibodies which fight food allergens.

When anyone intakes this food again, our immune system uses this antibody to fight against this allergen.

The European Union prepared a detailed list of allergens that identifies as wheat, rye, barley, oats, kamut, crustaceans, eggs, fish, peanuts, soybeans, milk, nuts, for example, almonds, hazelnuts, walnuts, cashews, pecan nuts, Brazil nuts, pistachio nuts, macadamia nuts and Queensland nuts, mustard, and sesame seeds.

Japan has declared allergens are eggs, milk, dairy products, wheat, buckwheat, shrimp/prawn, peanuts, salmon roe, soybean, kiwi, banana, crab, chicken, tree nuts, squid, mackerel, meat, salmon, gelatin yam, and peach.

TECHNICAL DICTIONARY

Here is the description of terms underlined in blue.

Food fraud: All the live animals that grow to produce food products are called livestock. For example, Cow, Goat, Pig, Chicken, etc.θ

Food defense: It is the growing of water animals such as fish or plants in the water.

<u>Back to top</u>

CHAPTER 6

FMCG New Normal >New Normal Emerging Trends

The "new normal" isn't necessarily a business world without working in an office; it's just a world where we focus on work rather than office space.

Bhavin Turakhia, Flock

The FMCG New Normal

The COVID-19 era was the most affected period of the century.

In most countries, people's lives worldwide have been lost due to the recession, which has badly impacted many industries.

This unique pandemic has changed the lifestyle in every aspect of life; people have changed their way of living by looking into alternate options that they had never explored before or thought opted for due to the ease of the business.

FMCG industries found their supply chain is broken. The plant was shut down, and the means of transportation were closed.

Making the availability of consumer goods to end-users became a significant challenge.

There also turns out to be a significant polarization of the spending power of all income classes.

Social distancing became a foremost mantra for keeping you safe from this deadly disease.

People are only willing to buy consumer goods directly once and unless it is proven safe by the vendor and the consumer feels safe.

Each FMCG brand's recovery path would depend upon how they are affected due to Covid-19.

The personal care products business also suffers significantly from people working from home, hence less consuming these category products.

There is a need to cope with this extreme level of market volatility.

In the current scenario, there is more thrust on preserving cash and net profit rather than looking into percentage margin.

During this period, offline purchases became weaker and weaker. The hotel & restaurant business suffers a significant setback worldwide due to fewer outings and restricted national and international travel; people opt for more creativity and innovation at home.

Let us discuss the emerging trend in the new normal during the Covid-19.

New Emerging Trend: New Normal

- The positive trend in hand-washing and laundry business
- The tremendous growth in E-Commerce /online business
- Change in the production planning cycle
- Increase in video conferencing and teleconferencing meetings
- "J" rise in work-from-home culture
- The trend to have high cash reserves with absolute profit
- Increasing the threat of online fraud
- Development of online delivery and store-on-wheel trend
- Polarization of spending power
- Increasing in live streaming sale
- Change in consumer purchasing behavior
- Preference for longer shelf life and more oversized packaging
- Increase in alternate brand trial

- Restriction in group activities
- Accelerated adoption of technology and automation across the FMCG industry

The positive trend in hand-washing and laundry business

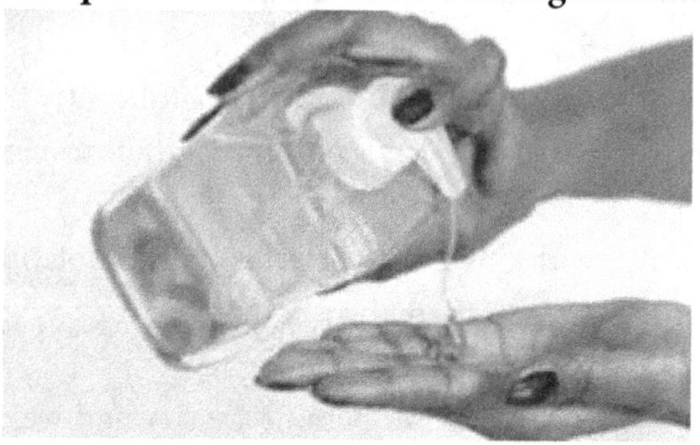

Hygiene has become a paramount priority across the world. With a focus on hygiene and health concerns by every individual in all age groups, the hygiene and laundry business sets in the pole position due to constant change in the hand-washing trend.

This business has changed the growth trend opposite before the COVID-19 era.

The tremendous growth in E-Commerce / online business

There is a significant shift from offline purchases to online purchases. Online business skyrocketed, whatever the growth rate achieved in a few months that could not have happened in the last ten years.

In Italy, online purchases increased by more than 200 %, which will continue globally for longer.

Online shopping and home delivery become the consumer's choice and, once it is sustained, will become part of daily life.

Change in the production planning cycle

There is a growing trend in the production planning cycle by shifting from a monthly to a weekly production cycle, producing only the biggest and most profitable SKUs.

Funneling out the most productive and profitable innovative products for new projects is an emerging trend.

It's nice to have turned into a must-have business priority. For example, sanitizer manufacturing was never Apple's eye-profitable product, but now it has become a premium product globally with a very high margin.

Increase in more video conferencing and teleconferencing meetings

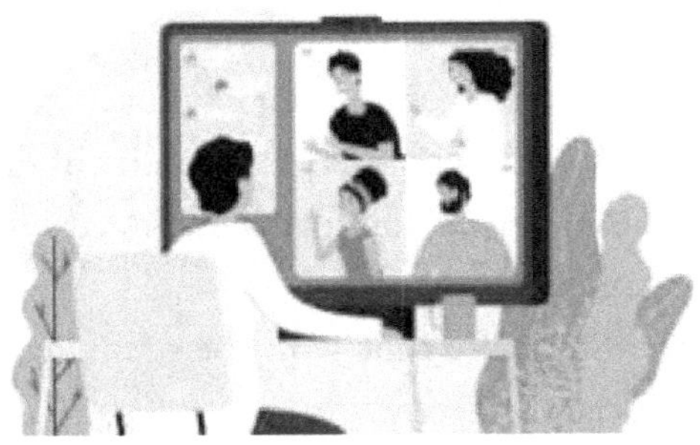

Since the arrival of COVID-19, there has been a rise in meetings through video and teleconferencing.

The traditional physical meeting has been replaced with an online discussion.

Geographical distance has been reduced to zero; the world is now connected on a single finger media click.

Various meeting platforms, e.g., Google Duo, WhatsApp, Webex meeting, Zoom, etc., are readily available.

It has drastically reduced the traveling cost and helped in fast decision-making, improving the organization's efficiency.

"J" rise in work from home culture

With the fear of the infection from the Corona virus, people have started working from home.

Most organizations encourage their employees to work from home without compromising the efficiency and quality of the work.

People are feeling more comfortable and safe working at home during this pandemic.

They are spending more time with their families and, at the same time, managing social connectivity.

It has helped in a drastic reduction in office and traveling expenses. Paperless culture is gaining momentum.

Telecom Industries are getting most of the benefits with this online working.

Nice to have turn into must-have business priorities

Many business opportunities that were the minor priorities in FMCG business have now become the top priorities.

Sanitization is one of the business opportunities that, before the pandemic, never appreciated and received a lukewarm response from top management, now turning out to be a premium product in the product basket.

The manufacturer has converted their units into more sanitizer-producing units and an enhanced capacity multiple times.

The trend to have high cash reserves with absolute profit

The market situation is very volatile; industries need to be more sure about the availability of liquidity due to a disrupted supply chain and need more confidence when the situation will be streamlined, and operations will be normalized and stable.

Industries are working to have more case reserves to face any adverse economic situation.

They are less supporting credit-based transactions and concentrating on absolute profit.

Increasing the threat of online fraud

With an increase in online transactions, there is also a sharp rise in online fraud.

People are suffering significant financial loss due to fraudulent calls in the name of a recognized brand, which is very difficult to track by ordinary people, and there is also a lack of an adequate legal cyber system to trap this network.

Although all the recognized brands are warning and helping people to be aware and keep themselves away from this network, now it is the responsibility of individuals to be alert and involved in only a safe and validated online transaction system platform.

Development of online delivery and store on wheel trend

Since offline purchasing lost its ground globally, FMCG businesses have launched their products to deliver to a consumer's doorstep efficiently without compromising the product's quality with a nominal service charge increase.

There is a rise in online order booking. The on-wheel trend is also increasing; there is no need to step out to market.

Grocery and food products are in high demand for these categories of services.

This concept is promoted due to work-from-home culture.

Polarization of spending power

The people's spending power is reduced due to an unpredicted future and the need to keep liquidity in hand.

Consumers have shifted their share of spending over grocery, staple, and health items.

There is a polarization of spending power all across the income classes.

The product will fetch the market, which offers value for the money to the consumer.

The organization has to monitor consumer behavior, re-evaluate the current market, and accordingly re-plan its product portfolio and position it with the correct value proposition and pricing.

Increasing in live streaming sale

There is a significant rise in live streaming sales; this type of sale is instant by offering a discounted-priced product for a limited period.

All the product features are explained instantly, and the buyer has to decide on a pulse rate and immediately purchase the product at home.

Change in consumer purchasing behavior

Consumers are forced to shift to online purchases as they do not have alternate options, but their purchasing behavior has remained unchanged.

Industries have to invest a lot to make this compulsion of online purchases into a habit; this is a challenging task but would take time to become a reality.

Preference for longer shelf life and more oversized packaging

With limited liquidity, uncertain future, and insecurities about a job, people are looking into purchasing products with a longer shelf life and products in more extensive size packages to maintain sufficient funds and reduce repeated purchases.

Increase in alternate brand trial

The shopping behavior of the customer is consistently changing; they are looking for a trial of alternate brands either due to the non-easy availability of the brand of their choice due to financial constraints or similar quality characteristics readily available in the alternate brand at a lower price.

Consumer goods manufacturer has to adjust its product production priorities to meet the changing consumer behavior.

The manufacturer has to change its approach from reactive to proactive as the current situation will not return to the pre-pandemic situation soon.

Restriction in group activities

There is a significant restriction in the group activities. For example, eating out, social gatherings, family get-togethers, enjoying long late parties, official customer meetings, etc., are no longer regular activities.

This trend will not return to the normal situation shortly.

People have to leave with restrictions.

Accelerated adoption of technology and automation across the FMCG industry

With restricted margins, reduction in profit margins, and a cash crunch situation, businesses are adopting new technologies and shifting towards automation in the FMCG industries to reduce the overall cost of production and improve operational efficiency.

Industries are also working on optimizing human resources.

Back to top

CHAPTER 7

Operational Excellence > Tools for OE in FMCG Industry

The reasonable man adapts himself to the world; the unreasonable one persists in trying to adapt the world to himself. Therefore all progress depends on the unreasonable man.

George Bernhard Shaw

Operational excellence Myths and facts

Operational excellence is a management concept of leadership, problem-solving, and teamwork that helps in the organization's continual improvement with a top focus on customer requirements, process optimization, and empowerment of the employees.

There are many pathways for implementing operational excellence and lean manufacturing; Six Sigma is one of those techniques.

How do we achieve operational excellence in the FMCG industry?

Effective and seamless implementation of an integrated business process is the key to attaining operational excellence.

There are many myths about operational excellence. People who found this difficult to implement raised many myths about this time-testing concept.

In this chapter, we have crosschecked every myth for not implementing it in the organization and busted these myths with detailed explanations.

Myth no.1: It applies to the manufacturing industry only

Myth-busting

OE is not only effectively implemented in the manufacturing industry but also in the non-manufacturing industry, such as the hospital industry, financial institutions, BPOs, the insurance industry, etc., where large amounts of the database are available for extensive analysis for continual system improvement.

You can see that none of the above industries belongs to manufacturing.

Deming's PDCA (Plan-Do-Check-Act) cycle is an efficient, systematic approach for resolving problems and continual improvement, irrespective of the industry.

Myth no.2: It is challenging to implement

Myth-busting :

OE just scared everyone because it is considered to be used purely as statistical tools only, such as Six Sigma, hypothesis testing, design of experiments, probability, statistical quality, and process control.

People do not want to learn this potent tool, as per their old thought of school, it would not add any value for the process improvements, and they stuck with traditional management by objectives methodology only.

Organizations are developing in-house operational excellence experts, like Six Sigma Green Belts, black belts, master black belts, lean, etc.

These trained people then enhance the skills of employees to improve each process by using simple tools like 5 S, Kaizen, Poka-yoke, OEE (Overall Equipment Effectiveness), 7 QC tools, etc.

Implementing these simple tools has helped in the visible, continual improvement of business processes.

Myth no.3: It is applied to a big organization only

Myth-busting:

It is happening because we hear success stories from big organizations only because it is more publically known to everyone and publicized by many consultant organizations, as well as the high revenue generation benefits fetched by these big organizations.

It is irrespective of the organization's workforce strength, the products it produces, or the revenue it generates. OE consists of standard tools and techniques that are applied to every organization.

It is a globally accepted concept that is relevant to any organization.

Myth no.4: Lack of resources to implement this

Myth-busting:

The organization is always believed to work in a routine mode, such as in firefighting mode, to resolve the issue and continue with the same, which is a never-ending process.

The organization's employees are busy with crisis management; they do not want to spare their employees for any new improvement activity as they think it is just a waste of resources.

The fact is that with the use of OE tools, organizations achieve excellent results and, at the same time, use those resources for setting higher benchmarking objectives for business excellence.

It is not a tool for reducing man resources but to upgrade the overall performance of employees and the organization.

Myth no.5: Everyone is doing, nothing new

Myth-busting

Some business organizations are fortunate to get good business results and satisfied employees and customers, and they claim to use operational excellence to get this result.

Operational Excellence In The FMCG Industry

It is altogether a different subject to discuss. In our earlier chapters, we have discussed the FMCG industry in FMCG (fast-moving consumer goods).

We have also discussed the food supply chain in our earlier chapter food supply chain and then various food product categories and the most popular foods, snacks, cakes, pizza, cookies, and biscuits around the world.

Since this is a significant global market with many challenges ahead for the sustainability of the business, there is a need for an approach towards business excellence.

In this chapter, we have covered each aspect related to Operational excellence in the FMCG industry.

This chapter consists of:

> **Operational Excellence: An Introduction**
> **Operational Excellence: Tools**
> **Operational Excellence: Benefits**
> **OE Tools Implementation**

Operational Excellence: An Introduction

Operational excellence is a management concept of leadership, problem-solving, and teamwork that helps in the organization's continual improvement with a top focus on customer requirements, process optimization, and empowerment of the employees.

There are many pathways for implementing operational excellence and lean manufacturing; Six Sigma is one of those techniques.

How do we achieve operational excellence in the FMCG industry?

Effective and seamless implementation of an integrated business process is the key to attaining operational excellence.

Operational Excellence: Tools

Alignment of the organization's strategy with vision using tools such as Hoshin-kanari strategy deployment, strategic grid, strategy map, etc.

Focus on delivering values that relate value to customers and the organization.

Active involvement of the leadership.

Engagement from top to shop floor employees.

High-performance team.

Implementation of cultural change.

KISS (Keep It Simple & Sensible).

Performance measurement of baseline KPIs (Key Performance Indicator) using BSC (Business Score Card).

Implementation of systematic PDCA (Plan-Do-Check-Act) approach.

Process excellence using lean Six Sigma methodology, 8D (Discipline) problem-solving approach, BPI (Business Process Improvement). DMAIC (Define-Measure-Analyze-Improve-Control), Kaizen, Gemba walk, TPM, lean VSM (Value stream mapping), 5 S, and many more tools.

Setting the benchmark (Sustainability and continual improvement).

Operational Excellence: Benefits

- Enhancement of supply chain management: Improved on-time delivery, lower inventory, better warehouse management, deep market penetration, etc.
- Product and process consistency and improved product

quality
- Improvement in operational efficiency.
- High loyal customer retention.
- Fewer sales returns and customer quality claims.
- Improved OEE of machines.
- Enhances employee skills.
- Excellent Data analysis capability and effective utilization of data for business intelligence.
- Effective and efficient R&D process with regular new product innovation and reduced time to market.
- More patented products.
- Enhance global presence, share, and sustainability.
- Cost optimization.
- Long-term business process sustainability.
- Efficient pricing and promotions.
- Efficient organization model.
- Enhanced value generation.
- International regulations compliances.
- Brand image

OE Tools Implementation

It is the methodology to achieve the objectives.

- **Effective deployment of business strategies**
- **Monitoring of performance management**
- **Attaining process excellence**
- **Highly efficient performing team**

Effective deployment of business strategies

Strategy deployment is aligning and linking business strategy and its execution.

Here are the following stages for this process:

- Organization of process
- Conducting a deep stick study of the as-is process
- Developing business strategic vision
- Developing breakthrough direction objectives
- Identifying strategic action plans and techniques
- Implementation of action and periodic reviews
- Hoshin-Kanri strategic deployment: It provides an organization with a proven and effective method to develop, communicate, and align the strategic objectives.

The Hoshin process is a systematic planning methodology to design long-term business objectives for up to five years with minor changes. It also keeps vigilance over day-to-day business activity measures to maintain the successful running of the business.

This methodology provides:

- Breakthrough objective focus
- Development of plans that adequately support the objective
- Review of the progress of these plans
- Changes to plans as required
- Continuous improvement of key business processes
- A vehicle for organizational learning.

This process is suited to the TQM methodology. The plan-do-study-act process improvement cycle repeatedly appears in the development, implementation, and review stages.

This cycle makes the following:

- Systematically development of the Plans
- Monitoring the progress of the plans
- Necessary changes in the plan as and when needed
- Attainment of the business objectives
- Standardization of the planning process

- Continual improvement in the planning process
- Improvement in the organization's learning curve

Monitoring of performance management

It is converting business strategic initiatives into measurable objectives and goals.

BSC (Business scorecard) is a powerful tool for monitoring business performance. It is widely used by many business organizations across the globe.

A long list of benefits is available using this tool, as below.

It helps management to focus on the practical implementation of the business strategies.

Focus and alignment of an organization towards goals and objectives.

It helps an organization to understand the relationship between measures and performance.

It helps in improving the communication of the organizational priorities throughout the organization.

This tool helps employees understand and focus on organizational priorities and realizing results.

Attaining process excellence

Process excellence is a systematically designed, effective, and efficient management, supporting process, and value chain system essential to delivering world-class results.

These are the stages of attaining process excellence:

- Selection of the correct project.
- Selection and training of the right team members and team leader
- Identification of the proper methodology for implementation of the action plan
- Excellence in the management of execution plans
- Sustenance of results

Process Excellence Tools

- Lean Six Sigma methodology
- Lean VSM (Value Stream Mapping)
- TPM (Total Productive Maintenance) / Autonomous maintenance
- 5S
- DMAIC (Define-Measure-Analyze-Improve-Control)
- OEE (Overall Equipment Effectiveness)
- SQC & SPC (Statistical quality and Process Control)
- 7 QC tools
- 8D (Dimension) problem solving
- DOE (Design of experiment)
- SMED (Single minute exchange die)
- Kaizen & Poka-yoke
- Skill matrix
- QFD (Quality Function Deployment)
- Muda, Mura & Muri
- Daily management
- Process & design FMEA
- World-class manufacturing
- Business process re-engineering

Lean six sigma methodology

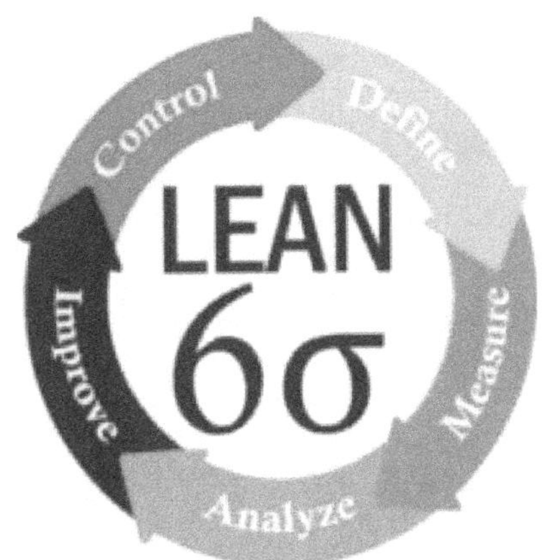

Lean and Six Sigma two are the time-proven methodologies many organizations use to drastically improve cost, quality, and time.

Six Sigma reduces process variation and improves output, whereas Lean reduces waste and improves workflow.

In the FMCG industry, for example, an inventory reduction could be achieved using lean tools, but process variation could be minimized using Six Sigma tools.

Lean & Six Sigma methodology comparison

Goal

Lean: It is to create a flow and eliminate the waste.

Six Sigma: Improves the process capability and eliminates variation.

Application

Lean: Primary manufacturing process.

Six Sigma: All business processes.

Approach

Lean Teaching principles and implementation based on the best practices.

Six Sigma: Teaching a problem-solving approach relying on statistics.

Project Selection

Lean: Driven by Value Stream Map.

Six Sigma: Various approaches.

Length Of Projects

Lean: 1 week to 3 months.

Six Sigma: 2 to 6 months.

Infrastructure

Lean: Mostly ad-hoc, no or little formal training.

Six Sigma: Teaching a generic problem-solving approach relying on statistics.

Integrated lean Six Sigma approach

Using Value Stream Mapping is one of the most effective tools to identify various improvement projects that can be accomplished using Lean or Six Sigma tools.

There is a need to educate employees in using lean principles to create an energetic work environment momentum and then slowly introduce the Six Sigma methodology later to address advanced problems.

Implementation of Lean Six Sigma depends on the specific organization's needs.

Some need basic 5S implementation, but some organizations have already implemented this and are looking to use the advanced Six Sigma tools.

Lean VSM (Value Stream Mapping)

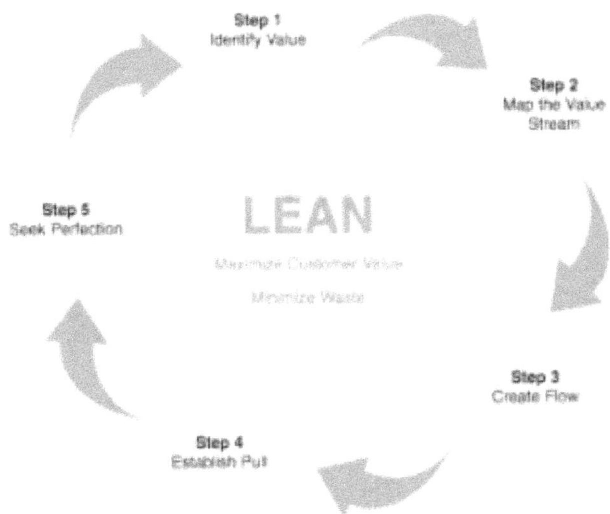

Value stream map (VSM) is a flow chart from raw material to final dispatch. In VSM, the person studies the whole process, identifies the non-value-adding process, and reduces that process.

It is a lean methodology with the primary objective of reducing or controlling waste generated during the whole process; this waste reduction may be due to overproduction, defective material, poor time management, poor transportation of material or people, high waiting time for getting instruction, etc.

The following are essential steps for successfully implementing value stream mapping:

- Identifying the scope of the value stream map
- Forming a VSM creation team
- VSM planning using the Kaizen tool
- VSM planning for process family by drawing process family matrix
- Identifying similar types of process steps
- Developing the current state map using VSM planning
- Starting by developing a basic VSM template

- Developing the future state map
- Developing a VSM draft plan

Following these basic steps and implementing them with the help of experts can be effectively implemented to get the desired results.

TPM (Total Productive Maintenance) / Autonomous Maintenance

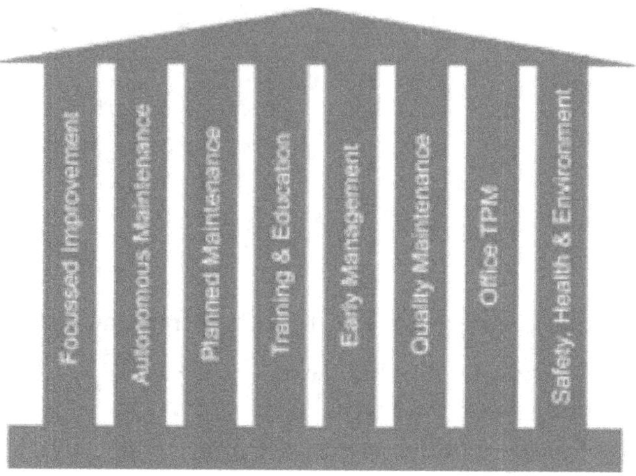

This tool is used to maximize the effectiveness and health of equipment.

TPM philosophy works on the fundamental eight pillars.

These pillars are as follows:

- **Focused improvement**

It measures losses, problem-solving, SMED, and OEE measurements.

- **Autonomous maintenance**

This tool is used to reset base level, inspection standards, 5 S, and setting standards.

There are seven stages of autonomous maintenance.

✓ Initial Cleaning (Initial Inspection & "Restoration"): Detect line problems and work to restore its original state. Cleaning and lubrication procedures are to be followed.

✓ Source of contamination and hard-to-access areas: Cleaning, Inspection, Lubrication.

✓ Standards of cleaning and lubrication: Developing tentative standards for cleaning, lubrication, and inspection.

✓ General inspection: This step provides inspection and autonomous skill training on equipment & products.

✓ Autonomous inspection: Develop a routine maintenance standard by the operator.

✓ Standardize autonomous maintenance operations: This standardizes routine operations related to workplace management, such as quality inspection of products, the life cycle of jigs and tools, set-up operation, and safety

✓ Autonomous management: Autonomous team working.

- **Planned maintenance**

✓ Reduction in downtime and initialization of condition-based maintenance.
✓ Training and skill development:
✓ Technical skill requirements know how to be developed.
✓ Initial phase management:
✓ Check specifications and technical evaluation.
✓ Quality maintenance:
✓ Reduction of defects and developing the operating standards.

✓ Work improvement:
✓ 5 S in the plant
✓ Safety and environment:
✓ Work towards zero accidents and zero pollution.

- **5 "S"**

The Five Steps of Housekeeping are as under:

✓ **Sort:** Separate all unnecessary items from necessary items and remove them from the workplace systematically.

✓ **Set in order:** Arranging all the necessary items in an order and keeping them in their designated place means a place for everything and everything in its place, using visual management. All required things must be labeled and arranged properly at storage.

✓ **Shine:** Clean everything, such as tools and workplaces. Eliminating stains, spots, debris, and sources of dirt is cleaning up one's workplace entirely so that there is no dust on floors, machines, or equipment.

✓ **Standardize:** Developing standards for educating at all levels for continual improvement. Standardization is maintaining one's workplace to be productive and comfortable by repeating 1, 2 & 3 "S."

✓ **Sustain:** It is training people to follow good work habits and strictly observe workplace rules. It means cultivating a disciplined work/ farm place where everyone does something independently to maintain a clean environment and understand the 5S philosophy correctly.

- **DMAIC (Define-Measure-Analyze-Improve-Control)**

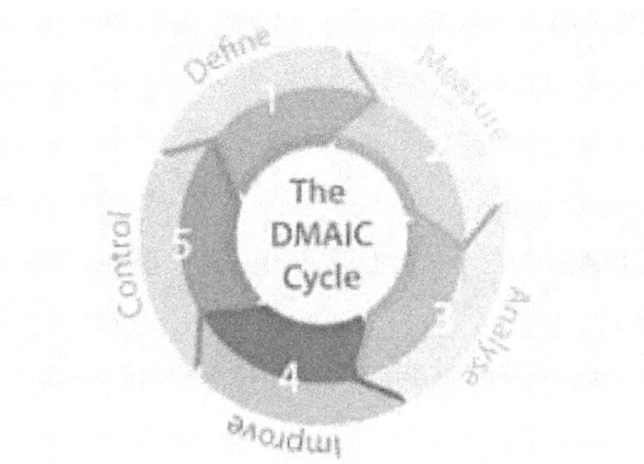

There are five basic steps in the successful implementation of Six Sigma.

✓ **Define:**

The purpose of the Define Phase is to determine the project focus.

- Develop Business case and team charter
- Map the Current Process
- Listen to the Voice of the Customer
- Define the Scope and Purpose
- Define the boundaries

- Expected resource needs
- Project Timeline

✓ Measure:

Collection of baseline data to identify the problem and its source of occurrence.

- Develop a sampling strategy.
- Validate your measurement system.
- Determine Process Capability and Sigma Level.
- Learning this concept and all applicable for collecting authentic and accurate data.
- A focused problem statement.

✓ Analyze:

- Process door vs. data door.
- To identify possible potential causes using $y=f(x)$ functionality.
- Developing an elaborate process map to do a value-added flow analysis.
- Find the change in which X's affect Y and in what manner, using Statistical Techniques.
- Ultimately, find which Xs are critical to moving the Y in the desired direction and at what level those Xs will be maintained.

✓ Improve:

- Evolve a practical solution that addresses the root cause of the problem.
- Evolve the "Should" Process and its potential impact (cost-benefit analysis).

- Assess risks and conduct Pilot Implementation.
- Routine implementation plan including budget, timeline, and responsibilities.

✓ **Control:**

- Develop Control plans and Control Charts to ensure that gains are maintained.
- Routine Implementation of Control Plan.
- Standardize and Document effective methods.
- Evaluating Results and summarizing key learning.
- Conduct revalidation when changes occur in the Process / Product.

✓ **OEE (Overall Equipment Effectiveness)**

OEE compares "actual output" and "should-be output."
It is maximizing the performance of equipment by minimizing losses of the equipment.

It is the framework for measuring the efficiency and effectiveness of a process through components of the process, that is, production rate, quality rate, and machine availability.

An OEE score of 100% means that we are producing 100 % quality products with 100 % productivity, and machine availability is 100 %.

The formula for OEE (%) is:

Quality rate (%) x Production rate (%) x Availability (%).

*** OEE is always measured in % (Efficiency).

✓ SQC & SPC (Statistical quality and process Control)

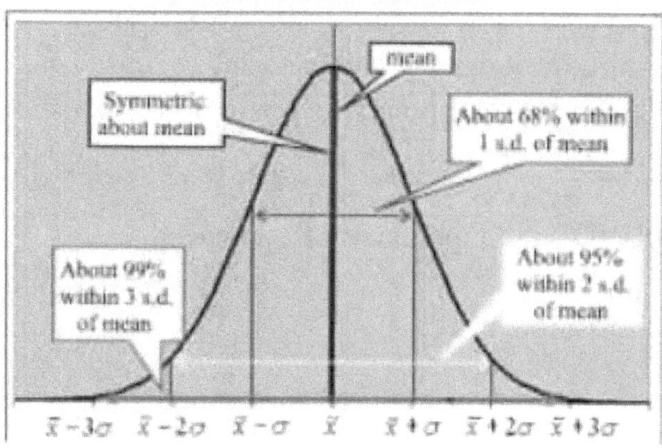

These are the two powerful statistical tools for different goals and requirements for any successful process application.

SQC tools are used for the acceptance of sampling.

It is based on consumer and producer risks, accept and reject the label, lot sizes, and a specific sampling plan. Sampling and acceptance of a given batch or a lot determine the final acceptance value.

The benefit of the SPC tool is that sampling is done at frequent intervals to increase the chance of finding a process problem in the early stages. It helps in making prompt decisions to arrest or minimize waste generation.

✓ 7 QC tools

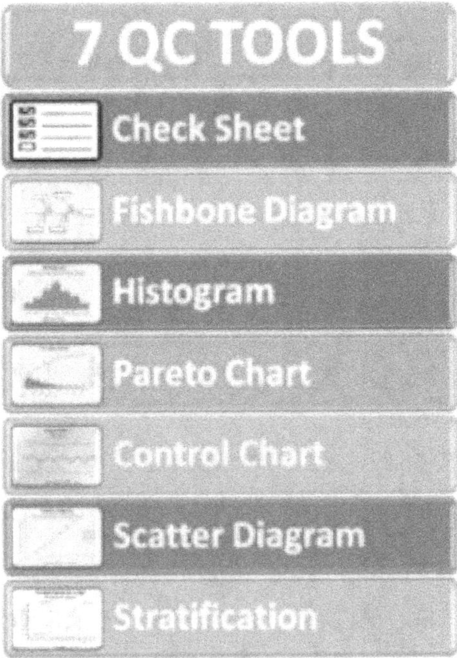

Seven QC tools are frequently used in many organizations to monitor and measure process performance.

- **Check sheet:** This is a tool to check the frequency of occurrence of any phenomena.

- **Pareto diagram:** This is based on 80/20 principles.

- **Cause-and-effect diagram:** This is used to the identified reason for failure.

- **Histogram:** This is a frequency monitoring tool to see the trend.

- **Control chart:** This chart monitors process deviation on a time scale.

- **Scatter diagram:** This diagram finds the relationship between the input and output variables.

- **Graphs:** There are various graphs used for monitoring and measurement of the process, such as bar graphs, pie graphs, etc.

✓ 8D (Discipline) problem solving

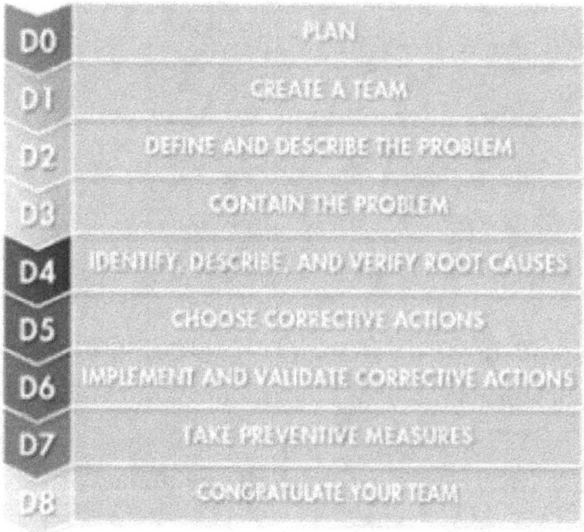

The eighth discipline is a typical problem-solving tool used in the industry by professionals.

The steps of this approach are as follows:

- D0 Plan: Planning and determining the prerequisite.
- D1 Use a team: Forming a team with process and product knowledge.
- D2 Drafting a problem statement: Quantifying the problem using the 5W1H tool.

- D3 Developing and implementing a temporary containment plan: This is to arrest any possibility of reaching the problematic products to the customer.
- D4 Identifying a permanent action plan to correct the problem identified.
- D5 Implement and validate the corrective action: The best-identified solution will be implemented.
- D6 Take preventive measures: This is to arrest the probability of recurrence.
- D7 Congratulation on success: Congratulation to the team for achieving success.

✓ **DOE (Design of experiment)**

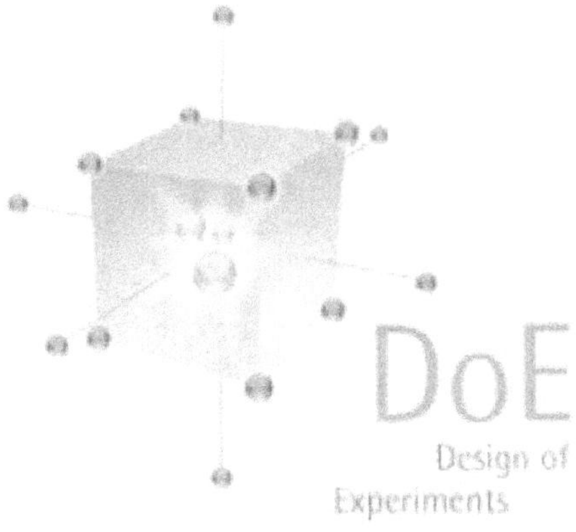

The design of experiments (DOE) is a powerful tool used to identify a specific factor influencing defect levels in the product.

The first step in applying the DOE principles involves identifying all possible factors considered independent variables.

Design of experiments (DOE) is a statistical tool for planning, conducting, analyzing, and interpreting controlled tests to look into the significant factors that affect the performance of a process.

It can be used in any situation in an experiment, possibly with a change in the level of a particular factor or multiple factors.

The basic requirements in using DOE for any process improvement that trials are being conducted should follow these rules.

Randomization: It helps in eliminating the effects of unknown or uncontrolled variables.

Blocking: It helps restrict randomization by only carrying out all trials with one set of factors.

Replication: It is a repetition of a complete experimental sequence.

✓ **SMED (Single minute exchange of die)**

This terminology comes from the goal to achieve the change over time to a single digit that is less than 10 minutes.

This tool is used for a dramatic reduction in time taken to change from one equipment to another or from one product to another, to do time study to take change over time from one product to another.

With this tool, change over to steps to keep it external while running the equipment and simplify and streamline the other steps.

The following are the benefits of the SMED approach:

- It lowers the manufacturing cost with fast changeover time.
- Fast changeover enables more frequent minor lot size product changeover.
- It helps in catering to customer demand.

- Small lot size results in low inventory level and inventory carrying cost.
- Flexibility in product planning schedule.
- Its smooth start-up results in process consistency and product quality.

✓ Kaizen & Poka-yoke

Kaizenis, made of two words, Kai (Change) and Zen (Good), means change for good, nowadays known as slight positive continuous improvement, which can result in significant major enhancements.

Three central pillars of Kaizen are as follows:

✓ **Gemba:** It is the Japanese word for the workplace. The team visited the site, identified an abnormality, and addressed it.

✓ **Muda:** It is the Japanese word for waste. Using Kaizen tools, the main focus is waste elimination, rework, process bottleneck, double handling, etc.

✓ **Standardized change:** The change was made using the PDCA (Plan-Do-Check-Act) cycle tool.

✓ **Poka-yoke** is the Japanese word for mistake-proofing or inadvertent error prevention.

It is used both in lean manufacturing and Six Sigma to minimize errors in the production process by preventing and resolving defects and eliminating the need for quality control during the production process.

✓ Skill matrix

This tool assesses the team members' skills, knowledge, and interests.

A table displays the person's proficiency level for a particular skill and knowledge and their interest in working on this job using these skills and knowledge.

There are the following proficiency levels.

- There is no skill at all
- There is basic knowledge of the task
- It can perform the primary task only
- It can perform all the tasks
- Can teach all tasks and train others

✓ QFD (Quality Function Deployment)

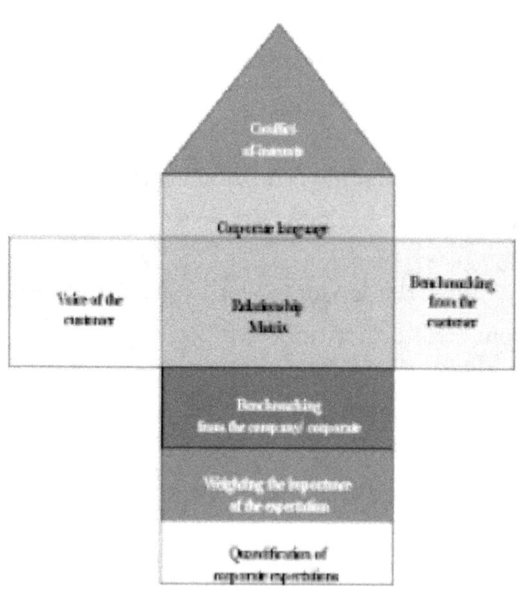

It is a methodology for listening to the voice of the customers and then responding to their needs and expectations.

Product or service quality is a measure of customer satisfaction.

The following are the steps for implementing QFD in the organization.

- To gather the voices of customers using an affinity diagram and tree diagram tool
- To build customer importance rating
- To develop customer competition rating
- Product specifications benchmarked against competition
- Developing direction for improvement
- Develop a relationship matrix between customer needs and plant capability
- Rating design attributes in terms of organizational difficulty
- Technical analysis of competitor's product
- Develop target product specifications
- Developing a relationship matrix is the next phase of the QFD project
- Calculating the importance of specifications

✓ **World-class manufacturing**

World-class manufacturing is the concept for many top organizations to become global leaders by being the best, fastest, low-cost producer or service provider.

This concept is beneficial for continually improving products, services, and processes to remain an industry leader and the first choice of customers and investors.

✓ **Muda, Mura & Muri**

Toyota has designed its lean system based on the elimination of Muda (waste), Mura (Unevenness), and Muri (Overburden).

There are eight types of Muda (waste).

Mura occurs due to fluctuation and variation in the various processes.

Mura and Muda's presence creates Muri among the employees on the shop floor.

✓ Daily management

The following are the steps of daily management methodology.

- Prepare & visualize standards for all 4 Ms (Man, Machine, Method, material)
- Defining standard work standards
- To have visual control of standards and results
- Focusing on the process stabilization
- Recording abnormalities
- Problem-solving
- Having a daily accountability process

✓ Process & design FMEA

It is a systematic approach used to identify risks in process changes. It identifies process functions, failure modes, and their effects on the process. Design inputs, if available, are to be included to study the impact on the end-users.

Each effect's severity is calculated using probability, occurrence, and detection.

Severity is measured by calculating RPN (Risk Priority Number). The severity ranking or danger of the effect is determined for each impact of failure.

By comparing the before and after RPN scores, a trend of improvement and risk mitigation could be chronically arranged.

Business process re-engineering

This tool recreates a core business process to improve product output and quality and reduce cost.

If this game-changer tool is used correctly, it can create a miracle in the business.

There are six basic steps for effective implementation of business process re-engineering:

Defining business process.

- Analyze business processes
- Identifying and analyzing improvement opportunities
- Designing of future state business processes
- Developing future state changes
- Implementing future state changes

✓ **Highly efficient performing team**

The essential inherent characteristic of a high-performing team is that it is a group with the right attitude, mindset, and competency level.

An organization with this type of team has the highest level of empowerment.

The capability of a high-performing team is that it is living with examples, breaking the organization's barriers, Business Analytics, motivating and result-oriented, and being an effective team coach and facilitator.

<u>Back to top</u>

CHAPTER 8

TOP FMCG AND PACKAGING TRENDS >Emerging packaging & FMCG trends

A hen's egg is, quite simply, a work of art, a masterpiece of design and construction with, it has to be said, brilliant packaging.

Steve Jobs

TOP FMCG AND PACKAGING TRENDS

In this world, change is the untold truth. Every next day, we are bringing new changes globally, as we all know that it is the survival of the fittest, and we have to be ready to adapt to the changes happening worldwide.

In this chapter, we are sharing top FMCG and packaging trends that are leading globally.

FMCG AND PACKAGING: TOP TRENDS

> Importance of the growing needs of sustainability
> The continual demand for transparency in the supply chain
> New trends of high barrier and coating technologies
> Focusing on lighter weight packaging

> The growing demand for easy to open the packaging
> To capture attention, customer convenience
> Close customer engagements and very effective promotion.
> Health and environment-oriented goods
> Use of advanced analytics for effective decision making
> Multi e-commerce channel and faster digital solutions

Importance of the growing needs of sustainability

As per the growing awareness globally for the reduction in the use of plastics and the use of sustainable, flexible plastic packaging.

Consumers are looking for sustainable packaging solutions and are ready to pay more for this kind of packaging due to more acceptance of social responsibilities, even in gift pack wrap, which has a concise shelf life and immediately turns into plastic waste as soon as a celebration event is over.

It has a significant environmental and business impact on companies and brands.

Consumer's purchasing decision is influenced due to growing awareness about sustainability.

Companies or brands should be very proactive in aligning themselves with this trend to sustain in a competitive market, or else they will lose business to their competitor. For them, sustainability is the top priority.

Continual demand for transparency in the supply chain

Now, a new trend is emerging for maintaining transparency in the whole supply chain of the organization.

Backward and forward traceability is gaining momentum, and food safety management systems already have this mandatory requirement.

Lack of transparency could lead to potential legal implications that no organization would like to afford.

The brands can improve their sustainability packaging by improving traceability throughout the supply chain.

The brand can communicate traceability to customers from procurement until the final dispatch.

Better product labeling helps the consumer /customer handle used packages; apart from this, the brand can help support the secondary use of the packages.

New trends of high barrier and coating technologies

Now, there is tremendous growth in the consumption of plastics and paper.

Sustainability has drawn attention to developing innovative packaging with minimum use of packing material with the highest barrier level and easy recyclability.

The coating is gaining momentum because of the shallow thickness (i.e., GSM). Globally but simultaneously carrying challenges for the direct food contact applications.

The solvent-based coating is no longer welcome globally; it is being replaced with environmentally free water-based.

Renewable resources, bio-degradability, and recyclability are becoming the new definitions in the FMCG industry.

Coating technology is the new niche specialty product segment for better business profitability and longer sustainability.

Focusing on lighter-weight packaging

The food and beverage industries are going through a challenging phase of business globally due to cost competitiveness.

Companies optimize their resources throughout the supply chain to reduce their final product cost.

Packaging consumes a large chunk of money. Final packaging is the major contributor.

In FMCG industries, when the cost of packaging a small-size SKU is reduced by a penny, it has a significant impact on millions of dollars due to a considerable volume size and large customer base.

Lightweight packaging is considered highly efficient; this addresses sustainability, durability, and excellent customer experience.

Throughout the package life cycle, light packaging helps be environmentally friendly, protecting product safety and flawless handling during transportation.

Growing demand for open-packaging

With technological advancement and spreading awareness for hygiene among all, working couples prefer more packaged food products that are easy to open, ready to eat, or prepared.

Opening the packed products has more significant challenges for the younger and older generations.

Manufacturers are continually working towards new innovative ways to ease consumers' lives.

Suppose brands need to look into a hassle-free opening solution. In that case, this will lead to customer dissatisfaction and will raise a threat to brand loyalty and shift to competitors if they find better options available to offer.

There is another requirement for packaging for the multiple uses of the same packaged product pack for repeated opening and closing.

Zipper and peel-able sealable pouches offer ease of operation and comfort.

To capture the attention of customers' convenience

Good professional organizations function like a customer service department.

Customer centricity is the new concept developing across the organization; this has opened a unique, exceptional customer experience in all aspects, where it deals with their business partner, i.e., supplier.

Customer loyalty is a significant factor as they have the option of multiple alternatives for the same kind of product.

There is a need for the business to reward their customer for their loyalty in the following ways.

- Home delivery
- Recommendation of the product with a personal touch.
- Wide variety of ready-to-go options.
- Rapid service chain of goods.
- Innovative experience for the competitive edge.
- Leveraging digital service for a secure, comfortable, and excellent customer experience.

Close customer engagements and very effective promotion

Nowadays, the organization has its branding strategy irrespective of the product and service it offers its customers.

Customers are already flooded with branding; this trend will continue in the future, too, with long-term engagement and innovative marketing techniques.

In the FMCG industry, prompt response, quicker delivery of short shelf-life products, and convincing the customers will challenge the marketing intelligence system.

The coming years will be an era of closer customer engagement.

We have to see how fast we are preparing for these challenges.

Health and environment-oriented goods

A single-use plastic ban sooner or later will become a reality.

Customers are becoming increasingly educated, and global food compliance rules are becoming stringent about the health and safety of the individual.

Social media plays a vital role in spreading awareness among people. If people found something wrong, they immediately raised the concern.

Products that have the feature of health and environment caring for individuals would be a prime priority product.

Paperless work culture and now single-use plastic ban drive heading towards a pollution-free, clean, and healthy environment.

We have a separate chapter on Single-use plastic.

Use of advanced analytics for effective decision-making

Globally, marketers, retailers, and manufacturers have understood the importance of data analytics.

They have started the use of advanced data analysis techniques for the growth of their business.

Using this technique, they are now accurately predicting the demand and supply of the products, customer expectations, and emerging market trends.

It is essential in the FMCG industry to predict the exact segment for promoting their product and generating sales revenue.

The following are the factors that must be considered while using data analytic tools.

- Online and offline commercial activities.
- Regular promotional and marketing campaigns to engage with customers.
- Tracking of all distribution channels.
- Automated real-time tracking of orders, sales, and distribution activities.

- Highly efficient and intelligent marketing team.
- Forecasting of future business scenarios using marketing or business intelligence tools.

Multi Ecommerce channel and faster digital solutions

One famous phrase is: "Where the sun cannot reach, the poet reaches there".

Now, the same is happening in the business. E-commerce has opened the Omni-channel to reach every corner of the globe, wherever the customer's presence exists.

Due to digital globalization, a wide gap between domestic and overseas customers has been filled up.

Customers are looking for the authenticity of brands before opting for the use.

E-commerce has given customers multiple choices, ease of secure online payment, and online or offline shopping convenience.

This multi-e-commerce provides convenience to the customer, the latest digital solutions for round-the-clock service, a strong presence, and, last but not least, personalization.

Back to top

CHAPTER 9

Global Food Safety Act >Major Food Safety Acts

A goal of the food safety professional should be to create food safety culture, not food safety program

Frank Yiannas

Global food safety act

In this chapter, we are sharing detailed information on Global food safety act

<u>This chapter consists of</u>

> **INTRODUCTION FOOD SAFETY ACT**
> **USFDA**
> **CANADIAN FOOD SAFETY REGULATION**
> **EU REGULATION**
> **REACH**
> **RoHS**
> **GERMAN FOOD SAFETY REGULATION**

> FRENCH AND ITALIAN FOOD SAFETY REGULATIONS
> JAPAN & KOREA SANITATION LAW
> CHINA FOOD REGULATION
> INDIAN FOOD REGULATION, FSSAI
> FOOD ALLERGEN
> FOOD COMPLIANCES TESTING INTERNATIONAL LABS

INTRODUCTION FOOD SAFETY ACT

Food is the basic necessity of every living being on this earth. People have been packing food for thousands of years to protect and enhance shelf life.

Until the last century, paper, ceramic, glass, and natural resin were the packaging medium for storing and transporting food items.

Since synthetic plastic material's invention, the definition of packaging has changed in this century.

With the invention of a wide range of plastics with different inherent properties, it is now possible to protect food from contamination and help enhance the product's shelf life.

Growing awareness for food safety among consumers also raised the bar for the demand for hygienic food; at the same time, in many countries, the government has developed their food safety regulations or adopted other country's or zone regulations to ensure that food reaches to the final consumer are safe without health hazards.

The food and packaging material's safety mainly depends on three critical factors.

These are the toxicity of the substances, migration of substances from packaging material into the food, and the level of exposure of these substances to food.

Standard test methods measure toxicity, while migration depends upon the type of food being packed and consumption by a person based on their eating habits residing in a particular region.

Due to the variation of this pattern, exposure is measured based on an average exposure model covering most of the population.

Some countries are very strict about the packaging system, whereas others rely more on migration data.

Regardless of the individual system, regulations authority consistently enforce standards to implement, and the industry has to comply with the applicable statutory and regulatory requirements.

The equipment and utensils used to prepare food restrict it, not the packaging material

In this chapter, we have provided information on various regulations established in multiple countries worldwide. These regulations include recommendations, legislation, or guidelines.

Many countries regularly update their regulations with new developments; for example, REACH updates its list of substances of high concern every six months and adds new substances every time.

Regularly visit the respective regulation's website for recent updates. Some countries publish many rules in the local language; here, we provide details in English only.

USFDA REGULATION

USFDA (United States Food and Drugs Administration) is an agency under the United States Health and Human Service Department that looks after the manufacturing and distribution of foods and other food streams of medicine, medical equipment, tobacco, and other consumer products.

Food contact substances

FDA uses the term "indirect food additives" when referring to migrating substances; The umbrella of FCS has identified these as Food Contact Substances.

These are the substances intended for use as a part of the material used for manufacturing, packaging, and storing foods but not impacting the final food quality.

Food contact substances are intended for use as a part of materials used in manufacturing, packing, packaging, transporting, or holding food if it does not technically affect the food.

Adhesive, film, ink, and paper are the food-contact substances that combine to make a food-contact material.

The FDA requires clearance for food packaging materials if the food additive definition is the food additive per the FDCA.

FCS has four sections:

- Food additives
- GRAS (Generally Recognized As Safe)
- Prior sanctioned
- Secondary direct additives
- Food Additive Regulations

Regulations are given in CFR (Code of Federal Regulations) under title 21, in "21 CFR – parts 174-18ummary

This information provided a beneficial overview of regulations applicable in the United States for food packaging material.

We must first determine whether the substance we want to add to our food packaging material is a food additive; if not, if it meets exemption, the substance is not a food additive. If the substance does not fit within the exemption, The FDA should premarket clear the food additive.

CANADA REGULATION

The Canadian Food Inspection Agency (CFIA)implements all health and safety standards under the Food and Drug Regulations.

Canadian food law: The following agencies look after the compliances.

Health Canada: This agency formulates the requirements related to health and safety under two rules (i.e., the Food and Drug Act (FDA) and the Safe Food for Canadians Act (SFCA)).

Canadian Food Inspection Agency (CFIA): This regulatory body takes care of the health and well-being of humans and animals and the protection of the environment.

Canadian Border Services Agency (CBSA): This agency ensures the security and safety of goods to and from Canada and enforces the requirements of the FDA, Consumer Packaging and Labeling Act, Canada Meat Inspection, Agricultural Products, and Fish Inspection Act.

Consumer Packaging and Labelling Act [CPLA]: This act covers the packaging, labeling, sale, transportation, and advertising of prepackaged products.

Consumer Packaging and Labeling Regulations [CPLR]: This act mandates bilingual labeling and units of measurement information.

Food and Drug Regulations [FDR]: This regulation advised the standards for the composition and labeling of food and drugs.

Safe Food for Canadians Act [SFCA]: This act takes care of food commodities, their inspection, labeling, safety, advertising, import, export, and interstate trade, developing standards for them, and other activities related to business.

EU REGULATION

The European Union now has 40 + member states. The EU 2002 established the first food safety law covering the whole food supply chain from farming to your dining table to maintain high food safety and health protection.

Every stage of the supply chain uses food contact material. Ensure the manufacturing, storage, transportation, and food handling systems are contamination-free.

These community regulations established are applicable as per framework regulation EC / 1935/2004, and at the same time, specific rules apply to certain materials or substances only.

Legislation on food contact materials is based on two basic principles: inertness and safety.

This framework regulation EC/1935/2004 is the base legislation that covers all the FCM and articles.

A.   Framework regulations 1935/ 2004/EC

General safety requirements
There should be no release of harmful substances in the food, which may impact human health.

Food, odor, or taste composition should remain the same at an acceptable level.

There should not be food fraud.

EU authorized to take measures for specific FCMs.

Labeling requirements

There should be a clear name, address of the producer or seller, instructions, text for food contact or symbol, and language that could be understood.

Traceability system

There should be transparency in the traceability of the final product, right from dispatch detail to raw material vendors, and all records should be made available as and when requested.

Declaration of compliances

For specific measures, the producer should have written documents to confirm the product as per the applicable regulations. In case of the absence of the same, member states can follow national regulations for declaration of compliance.

This document as to when and demand should be provided to the competent authority by the supplier.

Safeguard measure

Here, state members can restrict or temporarily suspend authorized FCM and vice versa; the commission could take a call to withdraw the same or adapt some specific legislation.

Good manufacturing practices (GMP)

It covers our quality assurance system, quality control system, and manufacturing practices; we follow GMP stringently.

It mainly deals with maintaining the hygienic conditions of raw material storage, processing area, equipment, final storage, dispatch area, and supporting services, e.g., Restroom, canteen, change room, personal hygiene, etc.

EU Measures on Specific Food Contact Material (FCM)

EU 10/2011 regulations for plastic materials.

EU regulation 1616/2022 for recycled plastic material.

Regulation 450/2009/EC for active and intelligent material.

Ceramic directives(84/500/EEC) for a limit on Pb and Cd migration.

Directive 2007/42/EC directives for regenerated cellulose. Uncoated or coated with a plastic coating, this should comply with EU 10/2011 directives.

Epoxy derivatives regulations Regulation 1895/2005/EC) for NODGE, BFDGE, BADGE, etc.

Nitrosamines(Directive 93/11/EC) and their release limitations.

EU regulation when the material is not covered by directives materials is suggested to follow resolution Resap (Policy statement) no legal.

Resolution ResAP(2004) 5 for silicone

Resolution ResAP(2004) 4 for rubber

Resolution ResAP(2004) 1 for paper and board material

Resolution ResAP(2004) 1 for coating

The most common required testing in the EU market

Global migration testing: This test comprises different stimulant(s) and specific temperature and time testing conditions.

- Distilled water
- 3% Acetic acid
- 15% Ethanol
- 50% Ethanol
- 95% Ethanol
- Iso-octane
- Rectified olive oil
- SML (Specific Migration Limit): This test applies to the unique substance.
- Acrylonitrile
- Bisphenol A
- Formaldehyde
- Nitrosamines
- Melamines

- Caprolactam
- Total content test – residual test
- Heavy metals
- VOC (Volatile Organic Compound)
- Vinyl chloride
- Phthalates
- Isocyanates

DOC(Declaration Of Compliances)

According to EC 1935/ 2004, the manufacturer or distributor has to submit a DOC of the product or material directly coming into contact with food.

To issue such a declaration, supporting test results should comply with EC 1935/ 2004, and its directives should be included in DOC.

GERMAN LFGB

This food contact materials legislation (German food, feed, and commodity law) is the same as EU directives 1935/ 2004/EC.

LFGB Regulation section 30 prohibits material that directly comes into contact with food and is endangered to human beings due to toxicity or impurity in the material.

LFGB Regulation section 31 prohibits bringing material into direct contact with food.

LFGB Regulation section 33 prohibits misleading information on products the supplier shares.

BFR (Germany's Federal Risk Assessment Institute) has implemented EU directives nationally.

Material not covered in EU directives is taken into BFR plastic standard for evaluation. It considers (but is not restricted to) Silicone, rubber, paper & paper board material, and polymers.

FRENCH DGCRF

France has its national food regulation- Decree 2007-766, the same as EU directives 1935/ 2004/EC.

To prove compliance with regulations, Arretes provides the following directives

- Arretes du 02/01/2003 for plastic material
- Arretes du 13/01/1976 for stainless steel
- Arretes du 25/11/1992 for Silicons

It includes 2002/72/EC & 84/500/EEC and other EC directive requirements.

When the material is not covered under Arretes

DGCCRF (General Directorate for Competition Policy, Consumer Affair and Fraud Control, national authority) information notice 2004/64 compilation of French regulations & requirements on FCM on a national level.

ITALIAN REGULATION

Italy has its national food regulation- Italian Legislative Decree 777-1982, the same as EU directives 1935/ 2004/EC.

To prove compliance with regulations, the ministerial decree provides the following directives.

Ministerial decree 21/03/1973

Ministerial decree 04/04/1985

Ministerial decree 18/04/2007

Some material covered under DM 21/03/1973 is Plastic, rubber, paper & paper board material, regenerated cellulose, glass, and stainless steel.

The requirement for the Plastic is in alignment with 2002/72/EC directives.

JAPAN & KOREA SANITATION ACT

JAPAN

In Japan, food contact materials are regulated under the Japan Food Sanitation Act No. 233, 1947.

Materials are getting tested as per notice no. MHLW 370/ 1959 "Specification and standards for food and food additives."

Testing performed under this standard includes total lead and cadmium, Heavy metals such as lead, Potassium permanganate consumption, evaporation residue, other materials, and specific migration testing.

KOREA

In Korea, food contact materials are regulated under the Korean Food Sanitation Act No. 3823, 10 May 1986, and its subsequent amendments.

Testing performed in this act is the same as in Japan.

REACH REGULATION

REACH

The European REACH Regulation (Registration, Evaluation, Authorization, and Restriction of Chemicals) 1907/2006 ensures that we know more about new chemicals being used in the EU and restrict the use of these chemicals, which may negatively affect human health or the environment.

Applicable for:

The substance regulation applies to all the products that are sold in Europe.

Requirements:

Suppliers must inform customers if any listed Substances of Very High Concern are present in products/parts with a concentration of more than 0.1% weight/weight.

The list is updated every six months, mainly in Dec/ Jan and June/ July month.

Key agencies part of REACH

The European Chemicals Agency (ECHA).

The UK Competent Authority (CA) is located within the Health and Safety Executive (HSE), responsible for the day-to-day running of REACH in the UK.

RoHS DIRECTIVES

RoHS

The European RoHS Directive on the Restriction of the Use of Hazardous Substances in Electrical and Electronic Equipment (EEE) may adversely affect human health and the environment and sound recovery and disposal of waste EEE.

Many countries have implemented similar regulations, the same as REACH and RoHS.

Applicable for:

This regulation applies to all electrical and electronic equipment and products that have an electronic component sold in Europe and can be sold in Europe.

Requirements:

According to this Directive, they must eliminate the following contents from their products.

- Lead (0.1%*),
- Mercury (0.1%*),
- Cadmium (0.01%*),
- Hexavalent chromium (0.1%*),
- PBBs (0.1%*),
- PBDEs (0.1%*)
- DEHP (0,1%*),
- BBP (0,1%*),
- DBP (0,1%*)
- DIBP (0,1%*)

* Indicates maximum concentration values tolerated by weight in homogeneous materials.

INDIAN REGULATION

The FSSAI is a statutory body under the Food Safety and Standards Act 2006.

FSS Act, 2006 consolidates various acts & orders that were handled by multiple departments; these are as follows:

- Prevention of Food Adulteration Act, 1954
- Fruit Products Order, 1955
- Meat Food Products Order, 1973
- Vegetable Oil Products (Control) Order, 1947
- Edible Oils Packaging (Regulation) Order 1988
- Milk and Milk Products Order,1992
- The critical functions of FSSAI are as below
- Setting standards for food products
- Developing safe food practices
- Licensing food businesses
- Ensure compliance through inspections
- Testing foods for standards
- Training and building capacity
- Citizens Outreach

CHINA REGULATION

A wide range of regulations are implemented in China to ensure the safety of human beings consuming food products.

China food safety regulations: This regulation established the responsibility of producers and business operators for food safety during storage, transportation of food products, and food fraud management of specific food.

China food additive regulations: The approved food additives list is given under regulation GB 2760-2011. Food additives should not be used to cover product deficiency or to produce degraded food products.

China food contact material and packaging material regulations (FCMs) are regulated by the China Food Safety Law with the latest updates. Article 32 & 62 of this law restricts the importation, use, or purchasing of food-related products which do not comply with food safety standards.

China food law and regulation: China State Council published regulations on food safety law dated 31 October '19. It includes detailed rules for food surveillance, assessment, safety, inspection, import, export, etc.

China label regulation: All imported foods and beverages must have a label, mostly in white color and written in Chinese characters. The title must be approved by CIQ (China Entry-Exit Inspection and Quarantine Bureau).

China food import regulation:

All imports are classified under three categories: prohibited, restricted, and permitted. Vendors looking to import food first need to get a license to import from the government and register with CAA (Certification and Accreditation Administration).

FOOD ALLERGENS

Food safety is a significant global challenge; we have every aspect in detail in our other posts. Food safety challenges are one of these challenges.

The European Union has prepared a list of allergens that are identified as wheat, rye, barley, hazelnuts, walnuts, cashews, pecan nuts, oats, spelt, kamut, crustaceans, eggs, fish, peanuts, soybeans, milk, nuts, for example, almonds, pistachio nuts, Brazil nuts, macadamia nuts, Queensland nuts, mustard, and sesame seeds.

Japan has declared allergens; these are salmon roe, soybean, kiwi, banana eggs, milk, dairy products, wheat, buckwheat, shrimp/prawn, peanuts, crab, chicken, tree nuts, squid, mackerel, pork, salmon, gelatin yam, and peach.

Canada has declared a list of top 10 allergens: milk, eggs, mustard, peanuts, seafood (fish, crustaceans, shellfish), soy, Sesame Soy, tree nuts, wheat, and sulfites.

INTERNATIONAL FOOD COMPLIANCE TESTING LAB

There are many certified international accredited labs those test products for its different global food regulations compliance.

- Intertek lab
- SGS lab
- TUV Nord
- TUV Sud
- TÜV Rheinland
- Eurofins

- AGQ Labs
- CFTRI, India
- Analytical Food Laboratories (AFL), US
- QIMA
- CCIC Europe
- RPS Laboratories
- V Trust Inspection services
- NSF
- ARBRO

Back to top

CHAPTER 10

Food Safety Certifications >Various Global Food Safety Certifications

Quality in a product or service is not what the supplier puts in. it is what the customer gets out and is willing to pay for.

Peter Drucker

GLOBAL FOOD SAFETY CERTIFICATIONS

All food packaging organizations have designed a system audit process to ensure compliance concerning for the food safety regulations as well as operational excellencein the organization.

In this chapter, we have covered all Global food safety certification systems

<u>**This chapter consists of**</u>

> GLOBAL FOOD SAFETY CERTIFICATIONS: AN INTRODUCTION
> BENEFITS OF :FOOD SAFETY CERTIFICATIONS
> GFSI : GLOBAL FOOD SAFETY INITIATIVE)
> DIFFERENT TYPES OF : CERTIFICATIONS

GLOBAL FOOD SAFETY CERTIFICATIONS: AN INTRODUCTION

The food supply chain is nowadays becoming more complex, and the world's big food retailers and converters brands are mandating their suppliers to have food safety certifications.

The Global Food Safety Initiative Scheme is a well-established organization that recognizes BRC, FSSC, BAP, SQF, IFS, and many more systems.

The supplier has any of these certifications, signature the guarantee of international compliance with food safety standards.

GFSI has created confidence among the whole food supply chain for food, packaging, packaging material, storage, and distribution networks.

Other certifications, for example, ISO22000, Halal, Kosher, Soncap, etc., are not directly recognized by the GFSI scheme but are well accepted by the customer. Halal, Kosher, and Soncap are country-specific requirements like Halal for the Gulf, Kosher for Israel, and Soncap for Nigeria.

BENEFITS OF: FOOD SAFETY CERTIFICATIONS

The benefits of food safety certifications are as follows:

- It enhanced food safety practices at the manufacturing site.
- It has improved the ability of an organization to produce safe packaging, packaging material, and food.
- This has helped enhance the food safety knowledge of the employees on the shop floor and throughout the organization.
- It has helped in getting ready for the new regulatory changes.
- Global recognition of the organization.
- It reduces the customer site audit drastically.
- It builds confidence among the customer for the supplier.
- It is a commitment to food safety.
- It minimizes the cost of unsafe food in the food supply chain.
- It has helped develop a traceability system from the delivered product to the raw material vendor batch.

- It differentiates among the competitors.
- It helps develop the best control and knowledge over the process and products.

GFSI : Global Food Safety Initiative

GFSI is not an FSMS certification, but it has authorized many certifying bodies that provide certification to many client organizations that fulfill the GFSI benchmarking standard against food safety criteria.

Various GFSI-recognized food safety standard system certifications are as follows.

- BRCGS (Brand Reputation Compliance Global Standard) for Food Safety Issue 9
- BRCGS for Packaging and packaging material Issue 7
- BRCGS for Storage & Distribution Issue 4
- FSSC 22000 (Food Safety System Certification) Ver. 6
- SQF (Safety Quality Food) edition 9
- Global GAP (Good Agricultural Practices)
- IFS (International Food Standard) Ver. 8
- BAP (Best Aquaculture Practices)

DIFFERENT TYPES OF : CERTIFICATIONS

✓ BRCGS (Brand Reputation Compliance Global Standard) for Food Safety

BRCGS is a global brand-accredited certification body. This certification guarantees the consumer or customer the standardization of quality and food safety, as well as the manufacturer ensuring compliance with legal obligations and protection of the end consumer.

This standard certification is now essential for manufacturers, retailers, and organizations that provide food services.

This standard was published in 1998; now it has published 9th issue.

This standard is focused on the following.

Development of the product safety culture.

Guidance for developing a system for food defense & security.

To ensure global applicability and benchmark with GFSI.

A better understanding of the high-risk and high-care production risk zones.

This standard has a total of nine sections.

- **Senior management commitment**

For the effective and efficient management of the food safety systems and the development of a food safety culture, it is necessary to have a committed senior management.

- **HACCP Food Safety Plan**

HACCP (hazard analysis and critical control point) is a program designed by internationally recognized codex Alimentarius that helps to identify hazards and conduct a risk analysis to ensure that there is no threat to the safety, quality, and integrity of the products.

- **Food safety and quality management system**

This standard section explains how the company designed its well-documented and systematic management system for the best product and process control to ensure trained staff, safe products, and customer expectations.

- **Site standards**

This section covers readiness, cleanliness, and control of the site on pest control, food defense, food fraud, and site security.

- **Product control**

Product control requires allergen management, product testing, and food fraud prevention to ensure safe and authentic product delivery.

- **Process control**

Effective SOP, along with a well-placed HACCP plan, helps to produce consistent product quality.

- **Personal**

This section explains practical training, the best hygiene conditions, and the use of protective clothing.

- **High-risk and high-care production risk zone**

This standard part explains the product's susceptibility due to potential Pathogens and other contamination.

- **The requirement for the traded products**

In this section, the standards explained about the products not produced on the premises or those products are processed at the manufacturing site itself.

✓ **BRCGS for packaging and packaging material**

Packaging is an integral part of manufacturing and essential to every brand product.

Customer interaction with the product depends on size, shape, and color.

It is the GFSI-recognized first global standard for packaging and packaging material.

BRCGS is globally the first certifying agency for this standard.

This standard applies to all types of product packaging, whether primary, secondary, or tertiary.

This standard is divided into eight different production methodologies.

- Manufacture of flexible plastics
- Forming of rigid plastics
- Forming of metals
- Glass manufacturing and forming
- Chemical process
- Printing process
- Paper manufacture and conversion
- Other manufacturing

This standard has a total of six sections.

- **Senior management commitment**

For the effective and efficient management of packaging and packaging material, it is necessary to have awareness and commitment from senior management.

- **Hazard and risk management system**

HACCP (hazard analysis and critical control point) is a program designed by internationally recognized codex Alimentarius that helps to identify hazards and conduct a risk analysis to ensure that there is no threat to the safety, quality, and integrity of the products due to the packaging and packaging material.

- **Product safety and quality management system**

This standard guides in setting requirements related to the technical management of product quality and good hygiene practices based on ISO 9001 principles.

It includes product specifications, monitoring of suppliers, product recall, product traceability, and handling of incidents.

- **Site standards**

This section explains the requirements for the product environment related to cleaning, pest control, waste management, layout, and maintenance of buildings and equipment.

- **Product & process control**

This section has the requirements for the design and development of the product, its quality assurance, process control, inspection, and testing.

- **Personal**

In this section, it is explained about practical training, the best hygiene condition, and the use of protective clothing.

✓ **BRCGS for storage distribution**

This standard was published in 2006 and links the BRCGS manufacturing standard and end-users like retailers and food service providers.

The objective of introducing this standard is to ensure the integrity, safety, and legality of the food, packaging, and consumer products during storage and subsequent distribution.

This standard is applied to the organization of warehousing, packaging, and distribution of packaged or bulk loose foods and consumer goods.

This standard is divided into eight sections.

- **Senior management commitment, as well as continuous improvement**

For the effective and efficient implementation and constant improvement of the storage and distribution system, the senior management should be aware and committed.

- **Hazard and risk management system**

HACCP (hazard analysis and critical control point) is a program designed by internationally recognized codex Alimentarius that helps to identify hazards and conduct a risk analysis to ensure that there is no threat to the safety, quality, and integrity of products due to storage and distribution.

- **Quality management system**

This standard guides in setting requirements related to the technical management of product quality and good hygiene practices related to storage and distribution based on the ISO 9001 principles. It includes monitoring the supplier, product recall, product traceability, and handling of incidents.

- **The site and building standard**

This section of this standard ensures that the site is identified and maintained to protect and prevent any hazard to the products.

There shall be no compromise concerning the product's safety, legality, and quality. Site security shall ensure the safety and integrity of the product.

The staff facility should be such that to avoid any possibility of product contamination.

- **Vehicle operating standard**

This section of the standard ensures that the vehicle used for transportation is suitable and adequate for the purpose desired and maintained in good repair and hygiene conditions.

The process should be in place to ensure that the product during loading and unloading is secured from contamination and malicious activities.

It is also explained that all legal compliances are met with minimum risk of disruption of the services.

It is maintained if there is a need for a controlled environment of safety and integrity of the products.

- **Facility management**

This section of this standard ensures that suitably designed equipment should be used so that there is no product contamination.

Planned maintenance is in place, which is critical to product safety, quality, and legality.

All the critical control points (CCP) monitoring and measuring equipment are correctly calibrated to ensure product legality and quality.

Pest control and GMP are in place to ensure no product contaminations.

- **Good operating facilities**

The goods accepted should be as per product specifications only. Handling and movement of the product should not threaten the damage.

The product storage environment, for example, temperature, should adequately be maintained to ensure that there is no threat to the product quality, integrity, and legality.

Process control should ensure no physical, chemical, or allergen contamination and a product is used within the shelf life allocated.

- **Personnel**

This section of this standard ensures that the person working for the production of the product is adequately trained and competent.

Due to the risk of product contamination, personnel, visitors, and other agencies, e.g., service provider staff, follow site hygiene standards.

✓ **BRCGS Wholesale module**

This section of this standard applies to wholesalers only that store the products from direct purchase and are ready to deliver or collect.

During the certification process, the wholesaler must comply with all eight steps of storage and distribution.

There are two additional requirements for this module:

Purchasing – Branded products

The organization shall ensure that the products purchased for resale are safe and match legality.

The wholesaler shall have a procedure to approve and monitor its supplier and their products.

✓ **BRCGS contracted services module**

This standard section explains additional services storage and distribution agencies or operators provide.

Below is the voluntary service that could be taken under the certification scope.

- **Contract packing**

- **Product inspection**
- **Quality control inspection**
- **Contract chilling/ refrigeration/tempering and defrosting.**
- **Contract cleaning of basket/distribution container and roll cages**
- **Waste recovery and recycling**

Contractual packing

In this section, it is reviewed and specified that all contractual services should not create any risk to products; if it is there, then all necessary controls are implemented.

Contract packing (Repacking, assembly packing)

The legality of the products is to be ensured when there is a secondary packing, repacking, or labeling operation in place.

Product inspection

If product inspection services are hired, it is to ensure that the quality and legality of the product are undertaken using appropriate methods, facilities, and standards.

Contract packing (Repacking, assembly packing)

The legality of the products is to be ensured when there is a secondary packing, repacking, or labeling operation in place.

Quality control inspection

The quality control system should comply with and meet the customer requirements if it is managed by the company.

Contract chilling/ defrost/ freezing / high-pressure process operation

For this category of services, service providers have to ensure that it is as per product owner only and that safety, legality, and quality are as per specification only.

Cleaning of roll cages, baskets, and another container on contract

If equipment cleaning is outsourced, service providers must ensure no risk to the product operating.

Waste recovery and recycling

The service provider must take All safe hygiene care while handling waste or packaging for recycling or disposal, meeting all legal requirements.

✓ FSSC 22000

The world population is growing daily, raising the need for good and safe food products.

The FSSC 22000 certification system fulfills this requirement.

It provides trust in the food industry.

This standard was published in May 2019. This certification is valid for three years, subject to compliance during the following two surveillance audits.

The benefits of this certification are that it complies with the Global Food Safety Initiative (GFSI) benchmarking requirements and with relevant accreditation body requirements.

This certification is based on the following:

Standard ISO 22000 requirements for the organization in the food chain.

Standard ISO 9001 requirements.

Prerequisite programs (PRPs).

FSSC 22000 additional requirements as required by stakeholders.

A. ISO 22000:2018

To get certified for both FSSC 22000 and FSSC 22000- Quality certificate, FSMS requirements are laid down in ISO 22000:2018 standards that are requirements for any organization in the food chain.

B. ISO 9001:2018

To get certified for FSSC 22000- Quality certificate, QMS (Quality Management System) requirements are laid down in ISO

9001:2018 standard that is requirements for any organization in the quality management system.

C. PRPs

Prerequisite programs (PRPs), as referred to in clause 8.2 of ISO 22000:2018, are to be audited that are specified in the ISO/TS 22002-x series, NEN/NTA 8059, and the BSI/PAS 221 standards.

D. FSSC 22000 Additional requirements

Management of services

In this additional requirement, when external laboratory services are availed, these laboratories should be competent to deliver precise and repeatable results using validated test methods.

Product labeling

All the final finished product labeling should comply with all the applicable food safety regulatory and statutory requirements of the country to whom this material is being sold.

Food Defense

In this additional requirement, the organization shall have a system for conducting the threat assessment to identify the potential threat and a mitigation plan to address that threat.

Food Fraud mitigation

In this requirement, the organization shall have a system for conducting the food fraud vulnerability assessment to identify potential vulnerabilities and a mitigation plan to address that vulnerability.

Management of allergens (Food-chain categories C, E, FI, G, I&K)

In this additional requirement, the organization shall have a plan for the risk assessment due to the allergen contamination and control measures to reduce or eliminate this risk.

Monitoring of environment (Food chain categories C, I & K)

In this additional requirement, the organization should have a risk-based environmental monitoring program and control measures to prevent contamination from the manufacturing environment, including microbiological and allergen controls.

Product formulation (Food chain category D)

In this additional requirement, the organization should have procedures for using ingredients containing nutrients that hurt animal health.

Transport and delivery of goods (Food chain category FI)

In this additional requirement, the organization has to ensure that there is no potential for contamination of the products during transportation and delivery to the customer.

This standard applies to the audit and certification for food categories and subcategories.

Category A

Subcategory AI: Farming of animals for meat/milk/ eggs/honey.

Subcategory AII: Farming of Fish and seafood.

Category C

Subcategory CI: Processing of perishable animal products.

Subcategory CII: Processing of the perishable plant products.

Subcategory CIII: Processing of the perishable plant & animal (mix) products

Subcategory CIV: Processing of the ambient stable products

Category D

Subcategory DI: Production of the feed.

Subcategory DIIa: Production of Pet foods (only for dogs and cats).

Subcategory DIIb: Production of the pet food (for other pets).

Category E

Subcategory EI: Catering.

Category F

Subcategory FI: Retail/wholesale.

Category G

Subcategory GI: Provision for perishable food, feed transport, and storage services.

Subcategory GII: Provision for the ambient stable food and feed transport and storage services.

Category I

Subcategory I: Production of the food packaging and packaging materials.

Category K

Subcategory K: Production of the bio-chemicals.

✓ SQF (Safe Quality Food)

This certification scheme is being managed by the SQF Institute to control the food safety risk.

This system requires a rigorous system for managing food safety risks and providing safe products by the manufacturer in the food industry.

This certification is GFSI recognized; this certification helps in building confidence in the customer for rigorous food safety programs implemented by the supplier.

Benefits

Managing Risk

Developing a food safety management system provides a company with an effective system for food safety hazards by creating a culture for producing a safe product and continually managing, monitoring, and validating the management system.

Maintaining Current Customers

Having food safety management system certification helps sustain customers for extended periods. The customer may ask for the same if it still needs to be done.

This certification helps you stay competitive and get qualifications to work with global customers.

Increase in market reach.

Nowadays, all large retailers and multinational organizations are demanding this certification to qualify other organizations as a supplier on a sustainable basis.

It helps open ample global opportunities for the products of certified supplier organizations.

Ready for new regulations

This new version, edition 8, helps the organization prepare and comply with global food safety regulations, like the United States and its FSMA (Food Safety Modernization Act). This edition helps the organization in preparing to meet the FSMA requirements.

✓ GAP (Global Agricultural Practices)

It is a global trademark and voluntary standard for good agricultural practices (GAP).

This certification aims to have safe and sustainable agricultural products worldwide.

Many producers, suppliers, and buyers are harmonizing with this standard globally.

This standard is designed to ensure the consumers that food produced at the farm minimizes the adverse environmental impact due to farming operations, with minimum use of chemicals and a responsible approach for worker's health & safety and animal welfare.

This standard addresses environmental, economic, and social sustainability requirements for every on-farm process; it helps improve the safety and quality of food and non-food agricultural products.

This standard requires that the manufacturer shall establish a controlling and monitoring system.

Registered products are tracked to a specific farming unit from where it was produced.

This standard is flexible for the soil fumigation and use of the fertilizer but very stringent for the storage and residue limit of the pesticides.

There should also be a record system of how the product was produced.

- **GLOBALGAP** does not issue the certificates but has authorized some registered certified bodies.

Producers need an administrative system to track all farm activities to get Global GAP certification.

A wide range of GAP certifications across the globe is as below.

- **ASEANGAP**

This standard aims to improve the harmonization of the product standards and facilitate trade that has higher opportunities for other ASEAN countries.

- **Malaysia – SALM certification**

Malaysia has developed many voluntary farm certification schemes, for example, fresh fruit and vegetable sector certification (SALM), livestock certification (SALT), organic sector certification (SOM), and fisheries and aquaculture certification (SPLAM).

- **Thailand: ThaiGAP & Q GAP certification**

The Thai government has developed various quality and safety "Q" certification programs. This certification is designed for the safety of each food production stage, along with a "Q" logo used for all agricultural products, whether it is crops, livestock, or fisheries. The Department of Agriculture issues certificates like Q GAP, Q Packinghouse, Q Shop, etc.

- **Japan – JGAP certification**

Japanese producer's group farmed the Japan Good Agricultural Initiative (JGAI) in April 2000; agricultural products are produced by a common standard of good farming practices in Japan – JGAP.

- ### China – Green Food and ChinaGAP certifications

The Government of China has developed a state agro-product and food certification system in the food chain with two GAP programs for certification in farming.

- ### India – IndiaGAP

India's agricultural and processed food products export development authority has developed an IndiaGAP standard.

This standard aims to get benchmarked recognition with GLOBALGAP and look into an opportunity in the European market for Indian agricultural producers.

✓ IFS (International Food Standard)

This standard was developed by German retailers in 2002 called IFS (International Food Standards), which was later acknowledged and implemented by France.

This standard is a common tool for ensuring food safety and monitoring the quality level of retailer-branded food product producers.

This standard is applicable at all the food processing stages after agricultural production.

This certification is demanded by most of the German and French retailers of the other European countries.

This certification is currently being demanded from private-label food products suppliers only.

✓ BAP (Best Aquaculture Practices)

The Global Aquaculture Alliance (GAA): This nonprofit international association aims to promote the best aquaculture practices through educating, advocating, and demonstrating.

It is the leading organization for setting the standard for farmed seafood.

BAP is the world's most recognized third-party aquaculture certification body; it certified the entire production chain, which includes farms, processing plants, hatcheries, and feed mills.

GAA recognizes that aquaculture is the only means for a sustainable seafood supply and fulfills the world's demand.

This certification assures the retailers, food service operators, and consumers that aquaculture facilities follow responsible production practices.

This standard covers the following four essential aspects:

- **Environmental responsibility**

It ensures compliance with standards that address issues such as habitat conservation, effluent, and water quality.

- **Animal health and welfare**

It ensure the best practices in animal husbandry for controlling the disease.

- **Food safety**

This standard ensures that no banned antibiotics or any other chemicals are used and only approved chemical treatments are carried out in a controlled manner.

- **Social responsibility**

This standard ensured compliance with local laws for worker safety, child labor, and community rights.

✓ HALAL Certification

With this certification, the halal logo can be used, which helps the products' marketing capability in Muslim countries.

It helps improve the quality of the food or product and maintains a high level of hygiene.

The general requirements for Halal certifications are as follows:

Every food manufacturer or food premises should manufacture or sell only halal products.

The person applying for certification must ensure that the sources of their product ingredients are halal only. The supplier should be halal certified or supply halal material only.

The company must form an internal audit committee and appoint an Islamic executive to ensure full compliance with halal guidelines.

The product must be free from non-halal ingredients during preparation, handling, processing, packaging, and transportation operations.

Apparatus and manufacturing facilities at the premises must maintain hygienic conditions.

There should be a separate transport for halal products.

There should be excellent manufacturing practices in place.

All employees should get medical vaccinations, e.g., Tetanus.

Any worker who is sick and can affect the product quality should not be allowed to work on the premises.

Workers cannot directly touch the raw material, in-process, and final products.

For example, eating, drinking, smoking, and storing foods and medicines are strictly prohibited.

Religious worship items are strictly prohibited inside the manufacturing premises.

✓ Kosher Certification

Kosher certification ensures the product is pure, organic, and wholesome.

Kosher originated from the word Kasher, which means pure, and it is suitable for the consumption of human beings.

Kosher foods need to comply with Kashrut rules that have been written in The Torah.

Kosher foods are mainly classified into poultry, dairy, and animal products.

Kosher has standard guidelines for producing animal food products and utensils used for making these products.

Dairy products can not be mixed with animal products; even utensils should be separate.

All milk-based food products should be derived from kosher animals only; they should not contain rennet or gelatin, and only kosher-certified equipment should be used for processing these products.

All other foods like fish, grains, soft drinks, tea, snacks, eggs, and vegetables are classified as Pareve per Kosher.

These products should be processed in kosher-certified equipment only. Wines and ingredients should have their kosher origin.

People worldwide, regardless of their region, prefer to choose kosher products because they are considered healthy and pure.

Kosher-certified products are organic products that are free from harmful chemicals. There is full accountability and traceability in kosher-certified food products. Food products having Kosher labels are very safe.

✓ Soncap Certification

It is known as the Standards Organization of Nigeria Conformity Assessment Program.

This certification requires that every incoming material into the country should not be substandard or unsafe.

Any listed regulated imported product must undergo a product conformity assessment in the country of origin.

There are three routes for the certification and different documents in different ways.

Route A: This is for unregistered/unlicensed products (Conformity verification)

Each imported shipment requires inspection, sampling, and testing per applicable standards and FCL (Full container Load) stuffing supervision and sealing as per the risk assessment.

Route B: This is for registered (Registration and conformity inspection)

Here, product registration is done after the verification of the supplier, along with testing and assessment of the manufacturer's quality system during the factory audit.

There should be at least 40 % of sealed FCL consignment's inspection, sampling, and testing is to be done.

Route C: This is for licensed products (Product certification system)

Here, the registration of products is done after the verification of the supplier, along with testing and assessment of the manufacturer's quality system during the factory audit.

This licensing of products requires evaluation of the product that includes testing, factory audit, and regular surveillance for a minimum of twice a year.

The compliance with SONCAP requirements is fulfilled by issuing the following:

Product Certificate (Unregistered)

It is issued for every shipment and is valid for six months only.

It is for Route A only.

Product Certificate (Registered)

It is issued for one year and is applicable for route B only.

Product Certificate (Licensed)

It is valid for one year only and applicable for route C only.

Certificate of Conformity (CoC)

It is issued for every shipment.

Back to top

CHAPTER 11

Best Hygiene Practices> Let's be hygienic before eat

Compassion suits our physical condition, whereas anger, fear, and distrust harm our well-being. Therefore, just as we learn the importance of physical hygiene to physical health, we must know some emotional hygiene to ensure healthy minds.

Dalai Lama

Hygiene

The world has faced many pandemics in past years, and each one has created a panic situation across the globe.

We had overcome each challenge that came ahead of us.

In a fast few years, we have come across below challenges that have raised a significant threat to the life of human beings.

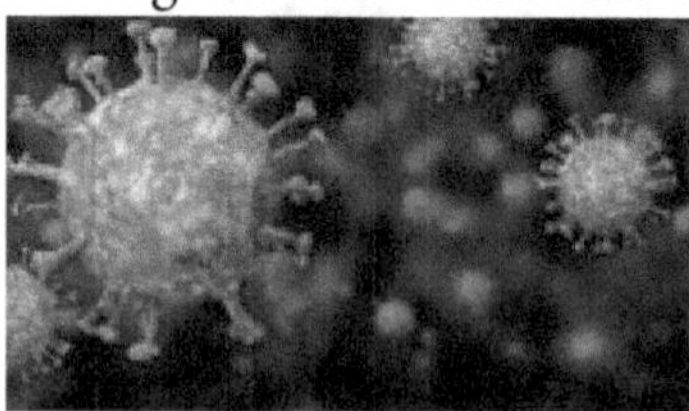

- Anthrax in 2001
- West Nile Virus in 2002

- SARS in 2003
- Bird flue in 2005
- Ecoli in 2006
- Swine flu in 2009
- Ebola in 2014
- Zika in 2016
- Corona in 2019 current challenge, and strain in 2020

Everyone has the right to get good quality, hygienic, and safe products. Good hygiene practice is the requirement to ensure that food is contamination free.

Food borne diseases could be due to the following reasons.

- Poor sanitation conditions.
- Lack of hygienic environment.
- Our poor hygiene practices.
- Sources of raw materials for food are unsafe.
- Our storage and transportation conditions are not hygienic.

The source of the unhygienic condition could be biological, physical, or chemical contamination.

Biological contamination could be from viruses, bacteria, or parasites that could present in the air, water, animal, food, and humans.

Out of three, biological infection is critical as it is not directly visible, but its impact is enormous.

We have been following hygiene practices for years everywhere in the world.

Our old generation is teaching these practices, and it is handover to the next generation to continue.

Nowadays, when we are on the verge of a significant risk of life threat with pandemic diseases, it becomes very immediate attention for all of us globally to follow the best practices available globally to keep ourselves safe from any life-threatening lifestyle.

The primary issue that needs immediate attention is increased levels of chronic diseases, mental health, obesity in childhood, and the aging population.

BENEFITS OF: BEST HYGIENE PRACTICES

✓ It enhanced best hygiene practices personally, socially, and at our professional working places.

✓ It helps in improving the overall ability of the individual and organization to be safe while using or manufacturing food products.

✓ It is a commitment of the individual, society, and organization to all the precautions everyone has taken to consider every hygiene aspect.

Good health and healthy products keep the cost of medication as well as the cost of unsafe food in the food supply chain.

Cleaning, maintenance, and hygiene helped in avoiding cross-contamination.

✓ It helps in reducing infectious diseases.

✓ It helps improve personal behavior like smoking, chewing, spitting, sneezing, coughing, etc.

✓ It helps in improving the excellent working conditions.

✓ It reduces food poisoning.

✓ You are keeping yourself and your workplace clean.

✓ Protect food from leading to illness or harm.

✓ Increase in the morale of everyone.

✓ Reduction in wastage of foods

✓ It helps destroy the harmful bacteria in the food while cooking or processing.

✓ It prevents any bacteria that enter the foods from multiplying to the level that could result in ill health or spoiling nutrition in the early stage.

Good hygiene is the prevention of the growth of the bacteria.

Increase the shelf life of the product as well as maintain the best quality.

A good reputation helps increase the business.

It keeps away pests from the food hence reducing food poisoning and contamination.

> **Best hygiene practice No.1: Rise early in the morning, at**

least 90 minutes before

sunrise.

Best hygiene practice follows the total enjoyment of the nutrient quality of the food.

The surrounding environment during this time is in its purest form, with the maximum amount of fresh oxygen in the air, which rejuvenates our body with new energy.

As per scientific research during this period, there is the highest level of oxygen (41%) in the atmosphere, which is very beneficial for strengthening the lungs.

Meditation during this period exalted all the poisonous chemicals from our bodies to keep us away from diseases.

People feel healthy, strengthened, and energetic. These people energized themselves with the first ray of the sum that cures many diseases.

Exercise in the early morning removes all body and mind stagnation, helps in reducing fats, and there is overall body comfort, another advantage of the early rise is that it helps in lowering BMI (Body Mass Index) means low obesity, fewer chances of diabetes, depression, or insomnia.

› **Best hygiene practice No. 2: Namaste (greeting)**

It is one of the most popular customs of India, followed from ancient times.

The meaning of this Namaste is that I bow to you and way of saying that may our mind is synchronized.

To perform Namaste, you must place the folded palms before your chest. It is the best hygienic way of greeting others, and to keep ourselves from such disease, we should also practice globally in the future.

› **Best hygiene practice No. 3: At home**

During the defection or urination process, wasteful odor generates, and we should our hands with cow dung ash till it becomes odor-free, or we can also use soap. It ensures that any modern hand sanitization liquid should be free from scent or color. It helps in removing harmful bacteria as well as keeping you hygienic.

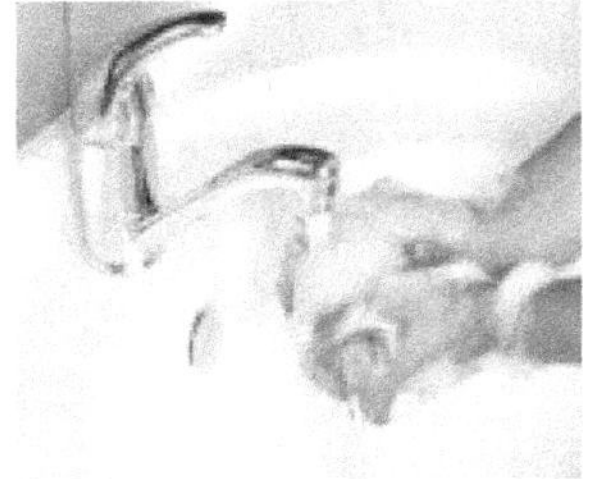

After that, there should be washing of feet and then rinsing of mouth as during the night sleep gas gets generated in our body that has to be removed by rinsing our mouth.

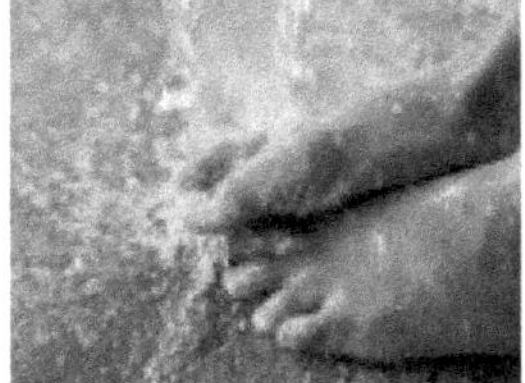

After that, we have to take water in a cupped hand to our face and eyes.

Regular cleaning of the teeth daily in the morning.

Take a daily bath early in the morning and wear well-washed, hygienic cloth before going for a morning breakfast.

Best hygiene practice No. 4: Fasting

In India, fasting has a long history; it is the country of yearly festivals. We celebrate with devotion, enthusiasm, and energy with social participation. God & Goddess are worshiped daily, along with a specific celebration.

There is a tradition of fasting during the festival to please the god or Goddess.

Primarily fasting is performed for 24 hrs, but it is subject to an individual's immune system for sustaining hunger and other medical constraints like blood sugar, etc.

The scientific reason for keeping fast is as under that is being followed for years.

- ✓ It helps in controlling and steadily maintaining blood sugar by decreasing insulin resistance.

- ✓ It helps in improving better health by reducing the level of inflammation.

- ✓ It improves heart health, improving blood pressure, triglycerides, and cholesterol levels.

- ✓ Due to less calorie intake, it helps in weight loss as well as enhancing metabolism.

- ✓ It increases growth hormone secretion, which is necessary for metabolism, weight loss, and muscle strength.

- ✓ It helps in delaying aging.

- ✓ It promotes the detoxification of the body.

- ✓ It helps in improving the immune system.

- ✓ It reduces the probability of health risks due to cancer. It promotes the detoxification of the body.

- ✓ It helps in improving the immune system.

- ✓ This reduces the probability of health risk due to cancer.

Best hygiene practice No. 5: Eating with hands

In Western culture, people hardly eat their meals by hand.

A spoon, fork, and knife are the tools used for eating the food, which is considered a well-cultured table manners.

In India and many Asian countries, Greek and the Egyptians, We eat food by hand only; although it may not sound good to many people, there are many benefits of eating it by hand.

Our fingertip represents all five elements: air, water, fire, earth, and space.

Our nerve ends at the fingertip help in boosting the digestion system.

✓ The finger is heat sensitive, preventing the mouth from eating hot food.

✓ It helps in eating slowly, which is good for digestion.

✓ Traditionally right hand is preferred for eating food, and one must thoroughly wash hands with soap and water before eating. It is a hygienic eating process.

✓ It enhances blood circulation.

✓ When we eat food with our hands, health-friendly flora protects our digestive system from external exposure to harmful bacteria. Using spoons and forks might contain home microbes and other germs since it is kept on the table for a long time and exposed to the external environment, which may contain harmful bacteria.

✓ One must wash his hands and mouth when he/ she finishes his food.

✓ Eating by hand gives a sense of fullness early, helping to eat less and lose weight.

✓ In another study, we saw that people using spoons, forks & knives, etc., eat very fast compared to people eating by hand may lead to blood sugar imbalance which may lead to type -2 diabetes.

✓ It helps reduce obesity due to controlled eating because by eating by hand, you consciously know how much intake you are taking.

> **Best hygiene practice No. 6: Camphor an environmental sanitizer**

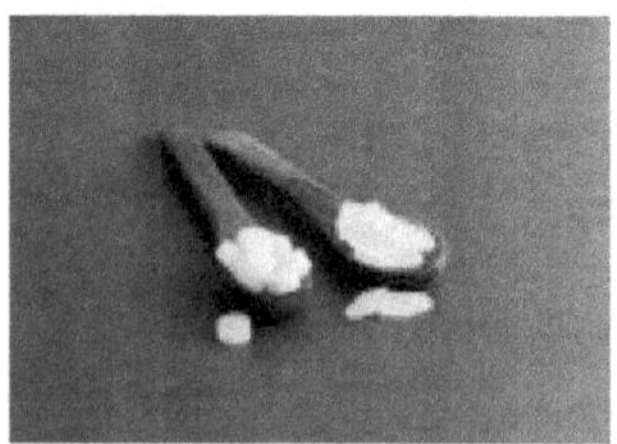

In Indian Hindu religious ceremonies, we have been using Camphor for years.

It is the last part of prayer when camphor candles and fumes spread in all the corners of the house.

The flame of the Camphor is Lord Shiva'sShiva's flame of consciousness.

From ancient times, it purified the air, and inhaling it has many medicinal advantages.

Camphor kills viruses and many other microbes.

Camphor is an active ingredient in the chest, muscular, and nasal ointment. It's another use as a moth and insect repellent.

Sometimes inhaling this and protecting against H1N1 (Swine flu virus) is suggested.

The substance present in this chemical is solid antiviral, antifungal, and anti-bacterial.

Best hygiene practice No. 7: Eating organic food

Fruits & Vegetable:

We produce organic food or food products without using any chemicals.

Chemical fertilizers, pesticides, and preservatives are not part of manufacturing organic food products.

Most of the population would like to know the benefits of organic foods, which is why it is more in demand and increasing daily.

Advantages of organic foods

We have better overall health due to no use of pesticides and other chemicals.

The use of organic foods leads to the intake of more nutritious antioxidants that help prevent cancer, vision loss, heart disease, premature aging, etc.

Grazing natural grass by animals provides heart-friendly CLA(conjugated linoleic acid).

Non-organic food sources, especially livestock, and feeds, use antibiotics, vaccines, hormone growth, and animal byproducts to treat and feed animals. When humans consume these products, this excess dose directly impacts or weakens their immune system, leading to less defense against diseases.

Organic foods are tastier than conventional food because crops take more time to mature and have all nutrients, minerals, and sugar structures.

No pesticides in organic foods save us from diseases like cancer, weakened immune system, congenital disabilities, premature death, etc.

✓ It is not a genetically modified product. The change in natural DNA produces GMOs (genetically Modified Products); this change might lead to slower brain growth, damage to internal organs, and thickening of the digestion system.

✓ It helps in minimizing the environmental impact.

✓ Organic foods are fresh as they do not have preservatives that enhance shelf life.

✓ There are fewer chances of foodborne illness.

✓ Organic food like milk has 60 % higher omega-3 fatty acids, vitamins, CLA, and antioxidants than no organic milk.

✓ Organic food products have a deficient level of toxic metals.

> **Best hygiene practice No. 8: Drinking water hygiene quality**

Water quality depends on pH, conductivity, minerals present, contaminations, etc.

Pure water is always odorless, tasteless, and colorless. It means good water should not have impurities like Total Dissolved solids (TDS); it is a measure of total ions, which makes water a good conductor of electricity.

Pure water is a bad conductor of electricity, but it is ideally not possible.

Drinking water is required to maintain good health; consumption varies per physical activity level, age, and environment-related issues.

As per WHO 2017 report, safe drinking water is a water source that does not create any significant threat to health when consumed over a lifetime, including different sensitivities that may occur during this period.

Benefits of good hygiene drinking water

As per science, we can not live more than 3~4 days without water.

✓ Using clean water keep us safe from diseases and hence reduces medical bill.

✓ It helps to maintain good health.

✓ It helps to produce crops contamination-free so that no bacteria or diseases spread while consuming these food products.

Water used for agriculture should be from safe and clean resources.

We have many hygiene practices earlier in this post, where there is a need for using safe and hygienic water.

✓ It provides nourishment. It is our life. Our body consists of 60% of water. Body hydration is mandatory for the effective working of the human organ system.

✓ It helps in blood circulation by carrying oxygen and nutrients to each cell.

✓ Unsafe water gives rise to diseases like Cholera, Typhoid, Hepatitis A, etc.

✓ It helps in getting rid of all toxins from our bodies.

✓ It improves sanitation because washing our clothes, body, and utensils and making our food with contaminated water will lead to diseases.

> Best hygiene practice No. 9: Reduction in food wastage

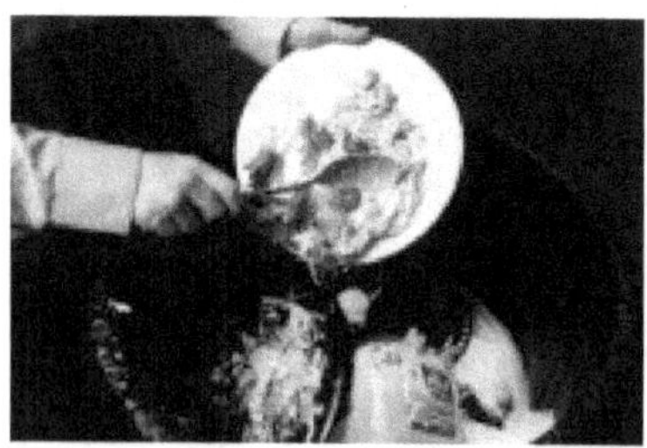

Food wastage is the food that remains unused after a certain period or is used for consumption but completely not eaten and thrown away as waste.

A complete food supply chain takes approximately 150 days from seeding to the dining table, but we discard the food in less than a minute.

There is an excellent impact on the water, land, environment, and biodiversity due to the wastage of food.

Impact of food waste on health hygiene

With the increased population globally, household food waste generation is growing daily. Unattended waste is a significant threat, and health hazard leads to the probable spread of infectious diseases.

Unattended waste is an attractive destination for flies, rats, and other animals that helps spread diseases.

Typically wet waste releases a lousy odor that leads to unhygienic conditions, thereby significantly threatening health.

> **Best hygiene practice No. 10: Product those enhance the immune system**

Many natural food products are available that help strengthen our immunity if these are taken regularly in our meals.

Current corona virus (COVID-19) outbreaks have forced us to remain fit and enhance the immune system that helps us I am fighting against bacteria, viruses, and Pathogens.

These products are as under :

Citrus food:

Grapes food, Orange, Lemon, etc., are excellent sources of Vitamin C. It helps enhance white blood cells level in our body.

Broccoli:

It contains Vitamins A, C & E, Minerals, fibers, and antioxidants. It is one of the healthiest food products.

Garlic:

It helps fight infection, reduces blood pressure, slows arteries' hardening, and boosts the immune system due to the sulfur-containing compound Allicin.

Ginger:

It helps in the reduction of inflammation which cures sore throat and nausea. It also helps in the removal of chronic pain and cholesterol.

Spinach:

It is high in vitamin C. It is a good antioxidant and contains Beta carotene, which keeps our skin and eye healthy.

It also helps reduce infection; it is always recommended not to cook thoroughly so that other nutrients get released from oxalic acid.

Yogurt:

It is rich in Vitamin D that is a natural defense against diseases.

Almond:

It helps in fighting against the cold. Half a cup of almonds is sufficient for the daily requirement of Vitamin E, as it strengthens the immune system. It is a fat-soluble vitamin because it requires fats to absorb Vitamin E.

Turmeric:

It is an anti-inflammatory compound in treating Osteoarthritis, and rheumatoid arthritis.

Green/ black tea:

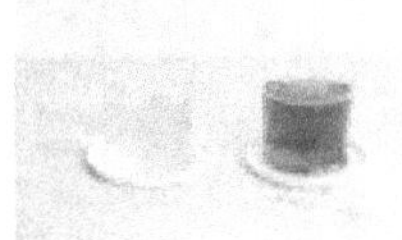

Both contain flavonoids which are antioxidants. Green tea also contains Epigallocatechin Gallate (EGCG), an antioxidant that helps improve immune function. It is also a good source of an amino acid (L theanine) that helps produce a compound in T cells that fights germs.

Papaya:

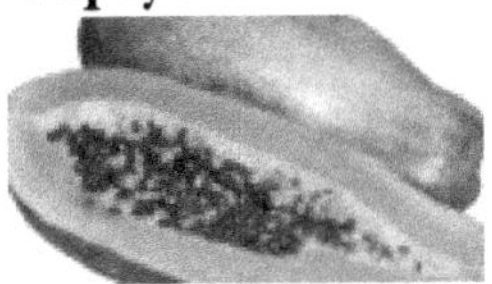

It is rich in Vitamin C. One whole papaya gives more than a day's body requirement of Vitamin C.

It also contains the digestive enzyme Papain which has an anti-inflammatory effect. It also contains Potassium, Vitamin B, and folate, which is beneficial for overall health.

Kiwi:

It contains Folate, Potassium, Vitamin K, and Vitamin C which helps in improving the white blood cell level to fight with infection.

Sunflower seeds:

It is a good source of phosphorous, magnesium, Vitamin B6, and Vitamin E, potent antioxidants. Vitamin E improves the immune system.

Back to top

CHAPTER 12

SINGLE USE PLASTIC >Recyclability and sustainability of plastics

Single-use plastic is a ticking time bomb for the environment. Avoid it wherever and whenever possible.

Jennifer Nini, editor Eco Warrior Princess

SINGLE USE PLASTICS

In this chapter, we discuss the pros and cons of Single-use plastics

Single-use plastic management

Single-use plastic or any other disposable plastic items are used only once and then are thrown as waste or sent for recycling.

It covers primarily plastic bags, straws, water bottles, and packaging material.

Around the world, approx. 300 Million MT of plastic are produced annually, and only 10-15 % is recycled. Currently, these are not biodegradable.

Now, we must look into more sustainable product options to 100 % recycle all plastics more efficiently and develop long-lasting value-added products for secondary application without impacting the environment.

Pros & cons of single-use plastic management

Pros:

Some medical items, such as syringes, bandages, applicators, and

drug tests, are used

only once due to contamination and possible infections. It helps in the prevention of the spread of diseases.

Some of the single used items can be reused and recycled for secondary, not critical applications.

This is being used for the addressing issue of wastage of foods due to spoiling, keeping them fresh for longer periods as traditional containers are effective in restricting wastage of food due to effective food processing techniques.

Around 20 to 30 % of food products go to waste due to the ineffective storage of the material.

Many prominent international players have set their target for reusable, recyclable, renewable, rechargeable, or refillable.

Due to plastic packaging, we could eat a wide variety of fresh goods all 365 days rather than in season only.

This highly hygienic packaging protects food products from air-borne germs and the spreading of these germs while handling goods intended for consumption.

It is versatile in many applications; it is peel-able & sealable to keep foods conveniently.

Cons:

Around 150 million MT of plastic waste is generated from a single use.

Approximately 90 % of plastics need to be recyclable.

Most of the disposal of plastics is through land filling and, secondly, through wastewater streams.

Micro plastic or micro-beads formed through break up or breakdown are not more than 5 mm in size and are not detectable; animal swells create health issues like intestine blockage and organ damage.

The human body creates a hormonal imbalance, infertility, cancer, etc.

Plastic is found in most water creatures in approximately 30 miles of area, a dangerous sign of disturbing ecological balance.

It also has an environmental impact due to the generation of GHG during manufacturing.

Single-use plastic management: Possible solutions

India is on the way to banning single-use plastic by 2022.

The manufacturer must rethink innovation in its design and sourcing of sustainable materials.

Apart from 3R (Reduce, Reuse, and recycle), there are 7R (Repair, re-gift, refuse, and recover). Repair means reshaping material for other uses. Re-gift means to pass on this item to someone else as a gift. Refuge means not taking plastic material like straws. Recover means up-cycle the material for recovering energy and converting waste plastic film into other plastic mold material or incineration for healing energy.

Needs to create a public education awareness campaign on purchasing reusable bottles using cloth bags instead of plastic grocery bags.

An Effective implementation of the extended producer's responsibility (EPR) system.

Plastic waste management should be integrated with the waste management of municipal corporations so that the value chain and current garbage handling system can be strengthened.

Instead of multiple polymer product type laminate plastic, single polymer type multilayered plastic is suitable for easy recyclability.

Reduce, reuse, and recycle of the waste (Waste management)

Reduce, reuse, and recycle, these three R's are the waste hierarchy.

These help conserve natural resources and energy and reduce landfills, allowing free space, sustainable life, and a pollution-free environment.

This campaign aims to reduce the waste of footprint and convert it into wealth through business.

First step: Reduce

It is the most preferable option to opt for waste management.

Avoid buying over-packaged items because this package will be gone as waste.

Use or purchase an item sufficient for our needs with no extra wastage.

To buy only durable products.

Reduction in wastage generation during processing at each stage of manufacturing.

Avoid using disposable items used for eating food products.

Proper packaging of food products during food processing has a high shelf life under good storage conditions.

By using the biological bag for purchasing the product from the market. Our old generation was used to this concept; this minimizes plastic bag consumption.

Purchase a perishable item in bulk quantity so that there would be less generation of carrying & packaging waste.

Second step: Reuse

Various first-use containers, like a jar, pots, etc., can store other products after proper disinfection.

Third step: Recycle

It is the step in which plastic waste like PET plastic bottles is recycled to convert into recyclable flakes for reuse.

Fourth step: Recovery

It is the step in which energy can be produced by incineration of waste in a controlled environment.

Fifth step: Landfill

It is the least preferred option for safe disposal of the waste.

Back to top

CHAPTER 13

SUSTAIANABILITY >Environmental sustainability

Earth provides enough to satisfy every man's need, but not every man's greed

Mahatma Gandhi

SUSTAINABILITY

By: Nitish Verma

Manufacturers in the flexible packaging industry are exploring various ways to drive sustainability in flexible packaging.

Extensive developments and machine trials are happening across the packaging value chain at different levels. Be it from Raw Material producers, Film Producers, or Convertors to Brand Owners, all are aligned and focused on how to make flexible packaging sustainable and eco-friendly.

Same polymeric family laminates, Monolayer laminates, Paper-based packaging, In-Mould labeled cups / glasses-based packaging, and +50micron thickness secondary packaging are a few of the areas where our Indian manufacturers are putting efforts to make the packaging sustainable and aligned with sustainability regulations.

Film producers play a vital role in this sustainability journey, having more responsibilities to develop specialty films /base substrates for any packaging evaluates for sustainable packaging.

Developing an appropriate film or base substrate for any downstream process is the first step to starting this sustainability journey.

Through this chapter, we shall look at various aspects of developments in film manufacturing as a solution to sustainability.

Any packaging primarily requires three main functional components:

> **Printability**

For identification of brand name, necessary information about the packaged product

> **The barrier to moisture and gas**

To maintain the shelf life of the packaged product

> **Sealability**

For intact sealing to ensure no leakage and contamination

Developments in specialty films for catering above three components:

Printability

Heat Resistant BOPP*films, as a direct replacement of PET layer from 3-ply laminates used as top printable layer responsible for only printing.

*Heat Resistance of >= 170degC exhibits good performance on packaging lines with no jaws sticking or wrinkles issues while packaging, especially in VFFS formats.

Based on application requirements, heat resistance is available in coating and uncoated versions.

Heat Resistant High Barrier BOPP*filmsas a direct replacement of PET layer from 2-ply laminates used as the top printable layer responsible for both printing and oxygen barrier

*Heat resistance as defined above; High barrier is through offline coating method achieving oxygen barrier nearly 100 ccs/sqm/day.

Surface printable BOPP* [UV and Conventional] films for monolayer applications. These films are for both packaging and label applications.

*UV printing is generally achieved by the offline coating method in BOPP. Monolayer films depend on application requirements and with Printing, Barrier, and Sealing attributes in a single film.

In-mould Label films is the emerging trend in India towards sustainability. These labels are fused with the plastic containers completely in the molding process itself, thus making the complete container recyclable. Surface printable IML exhibits good

printability with no littering of plastics, as it never delaminates from the container.

Barrier

High-barrier Metalized BOPP*films are being used extensively in biscuits packaging using 2-ply laminates. Such segment induced with a high heat seal and hot tack strength is required in candies, cakes, or other single-unit packs.

While non-heat sealable high barrier metalized, Bopp films are suitable for shampoo and chocolate applications.

*High barrier in metalized Bopp is available today with WVTR min 0.2 gm/sqm/day and OTR min 20 ccs/sqm/day. Also available with heat sealability offering SIT min 95 deg. C and Seal Strength 1.0-1.5 kg/25mm

High barrier Transparent BOPP films are suitable for see-thru packaging with improved barrier for enhanced shelf life.

Acrylic-coated films are generally used for good sealability and enhanced aroma barrier. Conventional BOPP films offer OTR 2000 ccs/sqm/day, while acrylic-coated films can offer OTR 800cc/sqm/day, which enhances the shelf life of the packaged product and retains the aroma flavor to a reasonable level.

PVDC-coated films are the preferable choice where an enhanced OTR level is the requirement. These films offer OTR in the 7-8 ccs/sqm/day range. Available in both BOPP and PET categories.

Ultra-high barrier Metalized BOPP films directly replace aluminum foil, offering barriers as low as 0.1, both moisture and oxygen, with much yield advantage over that of foil.

The density of aluminum foil is 2.7 gm/cc, while BOPP is 0.91 gm/cc.

Besides sustainability, the main USP of film Alu Foil replacement films is flex crack resistance that doesn't allow pinholes, safeguarding barrier loss.

Sealability

Acrylic Coated Films are suitable where exceptionally high seal integrity is the requirement in the packs. Acrylic Coating, when sealed through heated jaws, gets interlocked; hence, an airtight seal is formed. Acrylic-coated films are highly suitable for overwraps, especially in +50 microns, where heat transfer at the envelope sealing area is a significant concern due to multiple folds made. Besides, it gives an exceptionally high aroma barrier as OTR is almost 50-60% better than conventional BOPP films.

Low SIT, High Seal Strength*films are tailored BOPP films specially designed for high-speed packaging. Such films exhibit high hot tack strength, which is essential, while high-speed packaging, where the dwell time between packs and jaws is low.

*These films are available with an 80-85 deg SIT level. C, Seal Strength max. 1500 gm/25mm and hot tack strength max. 500 gms/ 25mm.

Above are a few of the thrust areas where film producers are meticulously putting their efforts; however, we are committed to creating more and more solutions for sustainable packaging and improving environmental performance.

<u>Back to top</u>

Epilogue

My lovely dear friends and passionate readers,

I am highly grateful to you for spending a perfect quality time reading this one unique book on altogether different kinds of genres right from the beginning till the end.

I hope this was an excellent experience for you.

I captured various dimensions of FMCG (Fast Moving Consumer Goods) terminology, Food Supply chain, range of Food safety challenges, , hygiene practices, and international food safety regulations and certifications, operational excellence, sustainability, etc. from different perspectives.

I'd written this book keeping in mind of global FMCG students and professionals to have a handy book for their immediate handy reference on latest FMCG development across the globe.

I had tried to captured every possible detail in a very precise way, but it might be possible that something had left right now, It will part of this book in the next edition..

Hygiene practices explained may feel uncomfortable to some, but it will give a second thought to think over there. There is no compulsion.

Various international food safety regulations will help to understand the gravity of food safety and approaches by different countries to ensure the good health of everyone.

We see everything in this world very simply, but to understand each, you should have different glasses to this highly complex world.

It was an effort to say a lot with a few words.

I explained all concepts in a familiar, easy-to-understand layman's language for my global reader.

I will wait for your valuable feedback to make this book more exciting, and informative. If you find some amendment are required,

I shall be back with updated version, and more interesting information; due to some constraints, I couldn't become part of this first edition, but, in a short duration, this would be part of the second edition.

Thanks a lot.

I am reachable at my Email: manish260470@gmail.com

Request please visit my website https://www.excellence2fmcg.com for more useful information on FMCG.

176

Back to top

Don't miss out!

Visit the website below and you can sign up to receive emails whenever Manish Sharma publishes a new book. There's no charge and no obligation.

https://books2read.com/r/B-A-IZTZ-RYYNC

About the Author

A seasoned chemical engineer with Master of Science from BITS Pilani. A Certified Six sigma Black belt.

CQI & IRCA qualified lead auditor for ISO QMS 9001, 14001, 45001, and FSSC 22000, IMS (Integrated Management System).

Diploma from IIP (Indian Institute of Packaging), Mumbai

A Competent professional with over three decades of industry experience in Flexible packaging, Labeling, Lamination, Chemical Production, Product Development, Project Management, Customer Relationship, Quality Assurance, and Technical services.

Skilled in implementation of lean methodologies and 5S technique;

Hold competency in food packaging grade product legal and statutory compliance.

And last but not the least the spiritual practitioner, who believes that life journey is always a path of new experience for betterment.

Read more at https://excellence2fmcg.com/.

www.ingramcontent.com/pod-product-compliance
Lightning Source LLC
Chambersburg PA
CBHW070516160726
48003CB00004B/1583